Do You Still Do?

WHAT HAPPENS HAPPILY EVER AFTER

Do You Still Do?

WHAT HAPPENS HAPPILY EVER AFTER

Cheryl Lacey Donovan & Keith Donovan

Peace In The Storm Publishing, LLC

Copyright © 2010 by Cheryl Lacey Donovan & Keith Donovan

ISBN-13: 978-0-9819631-2-9
Library of Congress Control Number: 2009922533

Peace In The Storm Publishing, LLC.
P.O. Box 1152
Pocono Summit, PA 18346

Visit our Web site at www.PeaceInTheStormPublishing.com

DEDICATION

This book is dedicated to the hundreds of thousands of couples who long to have a happily ever after but don't know how to get there. Keep God first and remember we don't battle against flesh and blood but against powers and principalities. It's the enemies job do destroy that which has been ordained by God. This includes marriages. Pray without ceasing, apply the Word of God to your marriage, and always keep Him first. Be blessed.

ACKNOWLEDGEMENTS

With love and appreciation we acknowledge the guidance and encouragement of our parents who helped make this book possible.

Our deep love, appreciation, and gratitude to our pastor Kirbyjon Caldwell who personally mentored us during some rough times in our marriage and to his wonderful wife Pastor Suzette Caldwell who taught us how to pray.

To Elissa Gabrielle and our Peace in the Storm Family, thank you, thank you, and thank you again for all you do to make these books happen. Your vision is one of true greatness and we encourage you not to grow weary in well doing for in due season you will reap a harvest of blessings.

To our children Christian, Francois, and Ashley, and our Grandson Caron, thank you for being patient, understanding, and encouraging as we fought our way through to develop a marriage of purpose that would edify and enrich each of your lives. We love you all.

To my husband, thank you. You will never know how much I truly treasure you. Thank you for praying for me and unselfishly supporting my ministry and encouraging me to fulfill God's purpose for my life.

To our Lord and Savior Jesus Christ, who is the author and finisher of our faith; we give all the honor, all the glory, and all the praise for our very lives. Without Him our marriage would be nothing and we render it a sacrifice unto Him.

FOREWORD

It's Friday, about ten in the morning, and I'm about to go on break at work. All I can think about is when I clock out for the day, the next time I report to work, I will be a married man. Although I love this woman very much and truly want to get down with her, was I really ready to commit to her and her two children? I'd grown attached to Christian and Francois but was I really ready to accept this challenge? I still remember the reaction I received from my mother and father when Cheryl and I started seeing each other on the regular, and things got serious. Both of my parents liked Cheryl from the start. She did a good job of making them feel comfortable, but the idea of me making her my main squeeze did raise question marks. I remember when Cheryl first started coming around more and more. I was still living at home with my parents, so when Cheryl would come over , naturally the boys were with her. Cheryl always made sure the boys were well mannered and she made it a point to show that she was an independent woman. But was I ready to marry a woman with two children who was coming off of a bad divorce? Only time would tell.

During the time Cheryl and I were dating I conceived a child with another woman. Shortly after Ashley was born I gave Cheryl al ring not really knowing what else to do. She was clueless about my daughter's birth. I didn't quite know how to tell Cheryl, but you know what's done in the dark certainly comes to the light. When Cheryl found out, we hit a rough spot in our relationship, but I knew I loved Cheryl and she was the one for me, after we reconciled once she found out about Ashley. That was the first of many signs of true love. But I still found myself questioning ; could this blended family work? Will we be this happy family all fitted together like pieces of a puzzle?

I really loved Cheryl and I figured it wouldn't be a problem. In my mind I thought, "I'm the man and it's going to work because I said it's going to work."
I was getting married in less than 24 hours and I started to realize my life was about to change forever.
That's a long time.

"Tonight's the bachelor party Dawg. We gon' get full tonight and send you out with a bang," were the words echoing loudly over the phone from my best friend Pat.

"Yeah Dawg. Let's do it," I replied. We'll get through rehearsal and dinner, but after that it's on. My bachelor party," I said to myself over and over again. I'd been to several bachelor parties in the past and I would always tease the groom to be about giving up his rights. In less than 24 hours, I would be the one getting the teasing.

"Okay, I thought to myself, let's see; got to pick up my tux, got to make sure one of my best friends is making his way down here from Austin, got to make sure Cheryl is okay, got to make sure everything goes as planned. Everything must be perfect." You pray that everything goes right for the wedding and that it goes off without a hitch. You definitely don't want to be the talk around the church or in the family if your wedding was unorganized and whack.

"A lot of preparation went into the actual wedding day itself with every detail being covered by both Cheryl and I (mainly Cheryl), however I would learn later that preparing for the wedding day and preparing for the marriage were two totally different things. We should've been preparing for the marriage. I know now why most churches require pre-marital classes before your wedding day. Even with the classes, if you have unresolved issues and demons in your life it's safe to say those issues and demons say "I do" in the wedding ceremony just like you do. Its extremely important that you and your spouse discuss every area of your life; children, discipline finances, habits, all up front. It took Cheryl and I years to understand that we were raised differently and neither one of us was right or wrong, just different. After putting GOD first in our marriage on a consistent basis, we both learned that her strengths were my weaknesses and my strengths were her weaknesses.

Most of us men like to live like we are happily married and we put on a front like we're handling our business. Don't let us be regular members of church or on the deacon board because we really put on a front when we are not truly right within ourselves. In reality, most men are insecure. We're only one trial or tribulation away from blowing our cover and losing it.

I remember several years ago, one of my co-workers told me about one of her close family members whose husband came home one day and said "Look, I can't do this anymore and I'm leaving you and our three children. I've already contacted the Attorney General so I can pay child support. You can have the house and your car, but I'm done. Outta here!!" I laughed at first especially about the dude filing child support on himself but then I thought this dude is a coward, how could he call himself a man and he's walking out on his family.

When our kids were young and all I was focused on was moving up the ladder and being able to provide for my family financially, I remember the constant tug of war between Cheryl and me as we tried to change each other instead of focusing on GOD. I remember feeling extreme anger when it seemed like nothing I did was appreciated. After going around and around with these feelings it became clear to me how a man could walk out on his family if he was not rooted in GOD.

Proverbs states that we must lean not to our own understanding but acknowledge God in all our ways and he will direct our path. In James Chapter 1 Scripture states that we should count it as joy when we have trials and tribulations because they help build our character. In order to have a successful marriage and not strangle one another, both husband and wife must apply these verses to their marriage on a daily basis. You must lean on GOD first before you lean on your spouse, and then as husband and wife, you build the character of your marriage by going through the trials and tribulations that come your way.

Most boys grow up watching other men in their lives and most of their values and morals are shaped by that person on a daily basis. Whether it's your father, uncle, big brother, older cousin, or a family friend, what we see and take in on a daily basis as a child will shape our character and play a major part on how we behave as adult men. In most cases, the married people in your family and the married people you knew outside of your family while growing up play a large part on how you will view your marriage.

Cheryl and I were headed for divorce court in a Corvette because we didn't prepare for our marriage as much as we prepared for our wedding. I thank GOD that we both agreed to see our pastor for marriage counseling because he helped both of us see that our problem was not that one of us was right or wrong, we were just raised differently. Not only that, we were not putting GOD first and each other second in our lives. Because of this, Cheryl and I were constantly at odds with one another.

The bible states that the two shall join and become as one. As a man and a husband, you must leave your mother's bosom and cling to your spouse. You must put GOD first in your life and focus on Him to give you strength. Most men love to quote the verse in the bible that talks about women being submissive to men. Sadly, most see that in a dictatorial way. However if you read the entire chapter, it talks about how the man must first be led by GOD. Are you being led by GOD? If not, that may be the reason why you're having trouble getting your wife to do things for you as a man. That's the reason you get frustrated with her and try to control her mentally, emotionally, and physically. She won't be submissive to you in any way if you keep trying to do it yourself. The good Lord is the only one who can truly change somebody's heart. Once I started focusing on GOD and trying to apply His word to my life, my relationship with Cheryl changed so much that it scared me. Every area of our lives had blossomed because we both decided to say "I do" every day. The Word tells me that a man that finds a wife finds a good thing. It also says a man must love his wife as Christ loves the church. Finally it states that a man can block his own blessings for not treating his wife according to GOD'S word.

Many years of agony and sometimes pure hell helped to build the character of our marriage. Deciding that we would never use the "D" word in our vocabulary helped to hold us accountable to each other. Deciding that we would truly seek to love one another and accept one another as God made us helped to bring joy to our marriage. Seeking GOD first as individuals has made it all work together. That old saying that being married is hard work and you must work at it every day is a very true statement. Marriage is work, but if you apply the right principles and put God first the reward is priceless.

I once heard my pastor say to us each morning you wake up the devil votes against your marriage. Each morning you wake up God votes for your marriage, each morning you and your spouse cast the deciding vote. The bible tells us how to live as a husband and as a wife, and if we do it according to His Word, our marriage will be blessed. The question is, what vote are you and your spouse casting each day?

INTRODUCTION

"Let's celebrate!" that's the message a wedding shouts to everyone in attendance. So we celebrate; sometimes even after the bride and groom have departed. We rejoice in the beginning of their new life together, hoping they will live happily ever after. But is that even possible?

The music fades and everyone leans forward to hear this beautiful couple's words of promise to each other. Standing before God, family members, and friends, they declare their love and commitment to one another. Fast forward thirty years and this now elderly couple enters the restaurant. They sit down to eat. The only conversation is the one held with the waiter. Living in a marital wasteland, they never exchange eye contact, never hold hands. Married for thirty plus years, they find themselves with an empty nest and no relationship because over the years it's become easier to focus on the aggravations, annoyances, and behaviors that frustrate and anger them in their marriage. They've lost sight of the significant gifts of kindness and service they receive from their spouse each day. Their critical negative attitudes have caused them to miss much of the joy of married life.

Society has done a wonderful job making us believe in the dream of happily ever after and a life of eternal bliss without true effort. What they've failed to do is tell us how to maintain it. You see, they don't tell you what it's like to wake up to someone else's bad breath each day or how to respond when the figure is replaced after forty or so pounds added after childbirth. Why do we spend more time planning for the wedding than we do planning for the marriage?

Great expectations are commonplace when we enter into a marital relationship but most of us are challenged when the reality hits our imagination head-on hurling us through the window of our soul to search for a soft place to land, only to find that there are chards of glass and steel waiting to cut us into shreds. Eternal happiness can only occur if two individuals are or become healthy on all levels; healthy enough to love unconditionally, healthy enough to be complete in their own right and healthy enough to trust God in all things including marriage.

What aids the process of becoming a couple? Why do some couples struggle? How can we turn that struggle into a victory? Keith and Cheryl Donovan have been married for seventeen years. But they've had to work hard and continue to work hard at building a marriage that glorifies God rather than each other. At times, resolve was the only thing that held them together.

Do You Still Do? is an insightful look into the realities of marriage. In it, Keith and Cheryl are honest

18

about their struggles and God's faithfulness. Because they want others to find real meaning in their marriages, the book equips couples with the attitudes, principles, and skills they need to have a fulfilling marriage of purpose and promise.

PROLOGUE

Black and white dresses with one long stem red rose for the bridesmaids and white calla lilies for the bride. My sister was one of the Maids of Honor and my sister-in-law was the other. I also had two Matrons of Honor, a junior bride, and a junior bridesmaid. My husband's best friend was his best-best man and for each bridesmaid I had, he had to come up with a counterpart. In the end we had a total of twenty-five people in our wedding party including two flower girls and a ring bearer. We were married in one of the largest churches in Houston by up and coming pastor Kirbyjon Caldwell. Our guest list contained over two hundred names, each of whom had been an integral part in our lives or the lives of our parents.

It was a warm April day and I arrived in the limo anxious to get started only to find out that one of the bridesmaids and her daughter who was a flower girl were late. Panic set in. But, my pastor, being the jovial man that he is allayed all of my fears when he made a brief appearance just before the ceremony to assure me that all was okay. This was a production of the highest magnitude after all. It would be several months later, when the videos and pictures arrived that I realized I left the sleeves to my dress at home.

The music filled the air with a melodious sound that brought comfort to my ears. One by one the cast of characters entered the sanctuary in perfect syncopation to the wedding music I had chosen; first, my mother and stepmother, then his mother. The bridal party followed close behind. Before I made my entrance the crowd was alerted by a "bell girl" who heralded my coming with the words "The Bride is Coming, The Bride is Coming."

That was my cue.

The doors opened and the view from my vantage point was simply breathtaking. Rose trimmed candelabras lined the pews. The flickering lights from the candles cast a beautiful aura throughout the room. Trembling legs and enough butterflies in my stomach to fill up the sanctuary my mind took flight. Am I really ready for this? I mean for years my husband-to-be had promised marriage but for just as many years he had kept his promise a secret from his parents. Whenever I talked about a wedding to them I was met with disbelief and trepidation. They obviously knew what I didn't. He wasn't ready for marriage. What makes him ready now? Did a lightning bolt from Heaven suddenly strike him and turn him into super husband? Or did he finally see fireworks? Why on earth do I want to do this again; because I love him? But in the words of the famous Tina Turner, "what's love got to do with it?" Would love really be enough? It wasn't in my first marriage.

What makes this time different? Can love really carry us into unmatched harmony?

The church was full of people waiting in anticipation. Each one dressed in full wedding regalia ready for the ensuing reception party. The two ushers unfurled the white carpet and quickly took their respective places. Apparently the angst I felt boiling over inside my heart had not made it to my face or surely someone would have said something. Even so, in grand fashion like the belle of the ball I stepped boldly into my place in front of the two large wooden doors making sure to grab hold of the strong arms that would escort me down the aisle. Our wedding had it all; beautiful music sung by the most angelic voices this side of Heaven, a heartfelt message delivered by one of the most prolific ministers of our time, and even the African tradition of jumping the broom.

My husband to be met me at the top of the stairs and graciously escorted me to our proper place in front of the pastor. I carefully surveyed the crowd and took inventory of everyone that was there. The lights were hot. I feared I might break into a sweat at any moment. The pastor proceeded with all the formalities as Keith and I stood at the alter boldly albeit robotically reciting our wedding vows; me in my white- fitted gown that hugged every curve to perfection reflecting my coke bottle figure, and my stunningly handsome husband – to – be whose white jacket with black trim showed off his "gymtastic" physique. The atmosphere was warm, joyful, and full of hope. Our love, we declared before the on-looking crowd with our ceremonial kiss, was all we needed to survive. Believing our wedding day passion would intoxicate us forever; we eagerly awaited the start of our lives together. What we didn't know was that the drunkenness of young love would soon give way to a hangover as the realities of life began to reveal themselves. Let the fairytale begin.

Before You Say I Do

Great Expectations

Once upon a time there was a little girl who found herself pregnant at sixteen. She married what she thought was her knight in shining armor, only to find out he was really the devil in disguise. The wolf in sheep's clothing almost swallowed her whole, but her savior on earth, her Mommy, saved her in the nick of time. Snatched from the jaws of evil, the little girl clicked her heels and found there was no place like the comfort of her mother's love. Determined to have a happy ending she whistled while she worked and gleefully returned home each evening. Then one day...

"I like jazz... how about you?" Those melodic words spoken by a man who was sure to be my junior because he still sang in the youth choir, fluidly oozed from his lips like one of the baritone saxophones playing in the background, he had definitely captured my undivided attention and I found myself absorbed in his every word. I had recognized him before; a medium height, well built bronze Adonis accused of resembling Mike Tyson, but much better looking and definitely better spoken in my book. Could it be that he was interested in me? Surely, this fine specimen of a man has a girlfriend or two waiting in the wings to answer his beck and call. He couldn't possibly believe I'd be swayed by his charming advances. Besides, I've sworn off men. They lie, they cheat, and they have no interest in marrying someone with two children already. I'll just keep my distance. But it's something about him; the eyes maybe or his boyish charm. You know they say the eyes are the windows of the soul. But what is his soul telling me?

Have you ever purchased a vehicle that you never really noticed before, only to find out once you buy it you see it everywhere? Well that's how it was with Keith and me. After that night in December, I saw him everywhere I went. It was crazy. I couldn't get him off my mind.

Spring had now sprung and even at choir rehearsal when I would attend with my good friend Kim, Keith was there. Okay, maybe I really attended so I could get a chance to see him, but still it was crazy. The music stopped and it was time for the announcements. The choir had several engagements for the upcoming week. Soon after all of the announcements had been made, the choir director dismissed the group and everyone made their way to their cars. After rehearsal, Kim and I remained and engaged ourselves in a conversation befitting two young women. We talked about young men. Almost intuitively Keith made his way into our discussion along with several of his friends. The attraction between Keith and I must've been obvious because slowly but surely, one by one , his friends excused themselves until Kim and I were the only ones left vying to maintain Keith's attention. The more we talked the more enamored I became. The three of us walked around the building several times hand in hand talking about nothing in particular. But somehow the only hand Keith's holding now is mine.

Spring gave way to summer and it was time for our church's annual family picnic. Unusual for a late August summer day in Texas the wind was blowing ever so lightly providing a soothing breeze for what was normally a scorcher this time of year. My sister Tanya, Kim, and I rode together to the picnic site which was traditionally in a small town nearby. As we made our way down the long stretch of highway in my little blue Chevette I made a quick glance to my right and spotted what looked to be a familiar figure stopped alongside the road. It was Keith and his girlfriend. His self- named vehicle, the Pony, (a white Ford Mustang), had a flat tire and Keith was working feverishly to repair it. I probably should've stopped but everything seemed to be under control. By the way, its worth noting here that even in that brief moment my keen sense of observation had taken over and imprinted on my mind's eye the matching blue and white shirts Keith and his girlfriend were wearing.

When the girls and I arrived at the picnic grounds we made our obligatory rounds and settled ourselves on a nice picnic spot near a large tree for shade. Keith and his date arrived a short time later but what stood out to me most of all about that day was that although Keith and I never really saw one another at the picnic we did more talking through my sister and Kim than I ever thought would be possible.

Go figure.

Six years later we were at the altar. This was my second marriage and my husband to be's first. Because I had never had a church wedding before , I, like most brides, wanted this one to be special. My first marriage was forgettable with domestic violence, drugs, and lack of support and I was all too ready to leave the past behind. But, getting married for a second time would prove to be more difficult than I ever imagined. Just as the Ten Commandments were emblazoned on stone tablets so were the terrible memories of abuse and betrayal from a marriage gone terribly wrong emblazoned on my heart. However, I scurried about and busied myself like a hamster on a wheel going round and round in circles with no real end in sight. Guest lists, honeymoon plans, caterers; this is what filled my days and my thoughts. So, the emotions from a long gone relationship stayed securely locked away in the vault of my soul.

Pre-marital classes were mandatory at our church but most of what was said was a blur. Family of origin discussions are the only thing I do remember. But it's safe to say that even the best prepared pre-married couples are ill-equipped for shaky finances, dual careers, old baggage and unmet expectations. Even under normal conditions the best relationships are in for big challenges. Add step-children and some baby mama drama and things can get really interesting. But, love for my husband-to-be and his love for me was all I cared about at that time. Love for one another would allow us to instinctively know what the other needed. We would be each other's source of happiness and as long as we had love everything else would simply fall into place, right?

NOT!

I knew marriage would bring change. Nonetheless, even expected change can be surprising and unknown. We were different. Our personalities echoed from contradictory voices. I couldn't get enough time with him; he couldn't get enough time with his family and the fellas. I liked people; he liked the people he liked. Our expectations were as far apart as the east is from the west.

Undying love, financial security, emotional fulfillment, what are you expectations of marriage? Ill-conceived ideas about what marriage is, tends to be the downfall of many relationships. Myths like "love is all you need" or passion will last forever are fables better left to the fairytales. Peeping into the windows of what were our parents' interactions with one another, our understanding of marriage was formulated in our childhood years. Silently we absorb these values, behaviors, and actions into our psyche only to release them as our marriages unfold. With broad brushstrokes associations create our portrait of the roles of husbands and wives. Previous relationships, friendships, society, religion, and other aspects of our culture also engrain themselves into our subconscious subtly coloring our outlook on marital interactions.

Emotional disillusionment in marriage is a symptom of lofty unattainable ideals. False beliefs about our spouse's ability to fulfill us will only leave us empty and dissatisfied. Scars left by deep and psychological wounds can't be healed by a spouse. Only the One who created you, the One who knows you can chisel away at the walls you've built around your heart and open the door once again to love. Acceptance, security, significance, and sense of purpose and worthiness are all deep personal needs that can only be attained through the love of God and self. God truly loves and accepts us as demonstrated in His Word.

Romans 5:8 But God demonstrates his own love for us in this: While we were still sinners, Christ died for us. He is the only one who can give us perfect peace. *Philippians 4:7 And the peace of God, which transcends all understanding, will guard your hearts and your minds in Christ Jesus.*

Mental, physical, spiritual and emotional completeness before marriage requires transparency achieved only through open realistic communication. Without it you and your spouse will become emotionless, withdrawn, and unhappy roommates with built up resentment which becomes insurmountable over time.

Knowing *who* you are and *whose* you are will quench your deep personal needs. Search for your true identity in the One by whom you were created. Truthfulness about yourself and dealing with the demons hindering your discovery will allow you to begin your marriage as a whole person not looking for someone to complete you but instead looking for someone to compliment you.

Acknowledgement of my incompleteness was a journey alone traveled. Having it all together was the destination at which I thought I had arrived. Little did I know there were many detours and stop signs ahead; roads to cross and hills to climb. Yes my journey was far from over and the only roadmap that contained the proper directions was my Bible. God was the tour guide.

Failure in my first marriage was not my fault but my relentless pursuit of perfection left me in a state where the agony of defeat was not an emotion I dealt with well. I propelled myself into a pace of perpetual motion like the earth rotating on its axis as I sought perfection in this relationship. As a woman, I needed to keep my family together at all costs; even the loss of my own personhood. Living a life full of hell and torment arguing and confusion was not something I wanted repeated ever again. Endeavoring, with all of my imperfection to be the perfect wife, anticipating my husband's every need, doing whatever was in my power to keep him happy at all times only exacerbated the problem. Confrontation was not an option (my previous marital confrontations had always been violent).

I was my own worst enemy expecting more of myself than I had to give. Ironically, this led to unimaginable conflict because I immediately became defensive the minute my husband expressed any dissatisfaction. My emotions were sensitive and easily damaged. I craved positive feedback. I wanted my husband to always look for the good in me regardless of what I was doing wrong. After all, I was making everything perfect for him and yet, he still found fault. It became apparent that my idea of happiness for him and his idea of happiness for him were two very different things. I was chasing my own tail trying to create an image of what marriage was suppose to be. Yet, in the process I was losing myself to the myth of marital bliss that didn't exist. Happy endings were only possible in fairytales and I was no Cinderella. Claire and Cliff Huxtable didn't live at my house and I needed to face my own demons if I was to move forward in my marriage to my husband.

Baggage I brought from my previous marriage was eagerly handed off to my new husband and I wanted him, no needed him, to carry it back and forth like a hotel bellman. But, Satan was packed inside each piece waiting for the perfect moment to jump out like a jack in the box and tear down what we were trying to build up. Neglecting to check this baggage at the gate threatened to destroy my marriage.

Doomed before he even got started by the memory of a neglectful, abusive, controlling, ex-husband, my new mate was facing an uphill battle. Scarred and afraid I went into my new relationship with preconceived ideas that turmoil was inevitable. These prejudices made me leery of all my husbands' actions and the walls I built up took years to tear down. So, it became a self fulfilling prophecy. Rather than wait on the turmoil to happen, I created it myself with unreasonable demands, clingy selfish attitudes, destructive criticism and defensiveness. Waiting for the fallout I readied my weapons, a sharp tongue and explosive attitude, and battened down the hatches.

Gaining insight into ourselves is always difficult. But dealing with emotional scars, deep seeded hurt and heartfelt disappointment in oneself and others can assure that you doom your own marriage.

The powerlessness, the anger and the guilt in my soul, all became my husband's to bear. My refusal to ever be the weaker vessel again made me fearful and apprehensive about letting my husband know I needed him; not for material purposes, but for support, encouragement, and unconditional love. I was unwilling to reveal the hurt, scared, little girl that was inside, so, instead, I became bitter, defensive, and controlling. Somehow I had unknowingly taken it upon myself to single handedly manipulate everything so that I would always end up the victor unscathed and unhurt. On the outside I was strong, independent, and self reliant. But inside, I was needy and dependent like a crack head on the corner waiting for the next fix, I was desperate for his approval and acknowledgement of a job well done.

Imagining emotional and psychological abuse suffered at the hands of my husband caused me to feel empty. My soul was bankrupt and in need of a deposit, but I had given the slip to the wrong person.

Understanding that God's grace was sufficient took some time. Only then was I able to let myself and my husband off the hook. I began to speak positive words about my husband. I focused on the good and not the bad. Before long our marriage began to change.

Challenging though it was, I had to learn to let go of past marital disappointments and learn to forgive, not only my husband, but myself as well. Willingness to let go of any unrealistic dreams and dealing with my own as well as my spouses imperfections was a positive step toward moving on.

Realistically, life happens. Perfection is an illusion chased after by only those who have deluded themselves into thinking it attainable. Financial situations arise, children go astray, and bodies will age and slow down. I wasn't ready for this; I wanted to live in a fairytale where conflict never happened. Healthy conflict continued to be an oxymoron in my world. When the situation began to disintegrate I really didn't know what to do next. Panic began to set in. I lost objectivity, communication ceased, consequently, in our early years of marriage the many methods of resolution we tried never worked. Our circumstances were deteriorating fast. Our most popular resolution method was Keith vehemently articulating his point of view and my retreating into myself and becoming defensive and resentful because I had mistakenly concluded disagreement meant a lack of love. Each time we argued my idea of flawlwssness was shattered by incongruity and I became frustrated, angry and drained. Life felt like it was caving in and we were on autopilot struggling to stay focused and incapable of making critical marriage-saving decisions. It took a long time to understand that a marriage without differences translates into one in which someone's opinions and ideas are not being heard; besides our critical resolution skills didn't solve the problem. But we didn't know what else to do. Culturally we had been geared toward seeing conflict as a competition to be won or lost. We had mastered all the rules for trashing our marriage, selfishness, picking at each other, my favorites letting the kids be more important and trying to be his mother, his favorites treating your friends better than your spouse and blowing up when angry, and downright refusing to meet each other's emotional needs. I regret to say that I became bitter toward my husband and our marriage. Although we could've given up on many occasions, we trusted in the Lord to carry us through the difficult years. Guess what? He did.

Not proud of the hardships endured early in our marriage, we can now look back on these trials as growing pains that prepared us for a greater life together.

"Consider it pure joy, my brothers, whenever you face trials of many kinds, because you know that the testing of your faith develops perseverance" (James 1:2).

Thankfully we all grow in life and Keith and I were no exception. We've grown in learning about each other and how to respond when we're involved in heated fellowship. As God's grace continues to raise us up we better understand the rules of engagement. We have learned when, where, and how to engage one another in communication that is edifying to each of us. Not unlike any other aspects of life our manual, the Bible, has given us the time honored biblical principles which have meandered their way into our disagreements. We now use them to sustain our marriage.

One of the most important principles we've learned and are still working on today can be found in *Proverbs 13:28 "the heart of the righteous weighs its answers, but the mouth of the wicked gushes evil."* Along the same lines Proverbs 13:3 says *"he who guards his lips guards his life but he who speaks rashly will come to ruin."* This means shut up and listen. But be careful that your mastery of "speaking the truth" doesn't become one sided as you are quick to point out anything you see or perceive in your spouse. Conversely, don't get stuck at the in love part of the confrontation and become completely accepting and tolerant of any behavior to the point that you become paralyzed with a fear of hurting your spouse's feelings. Withdrawal into you, passivity and silence are the only outcomes of this behavior. Speaking the truth in love combines both and allows us to confront unacceptable behaviors without compromise yet with absolute care and respect for each other saying things in a way the other person can accept. Taking a stance to live out Paul's challenge allowed judging and passivity to disappear.

Cutting better than any two edged sword my tongue could be a weapon of mass destruction. There were times when I was in quiet desperation because I believed I was right and Keith was wrong. I was wasting precious time trying to get him to see my views; besides that never solved anything. The word even reminds us in Galatians that if we keep biting at one another and devouring each other we will ultimately be destroyed. Galatians 5:15. These foolish arguments about things that don't even matter lead to the quarrels spoken of in 2 Timothy 2:23-26. You know the kind I'm talking about; the ones where a deep sigh or telling glance or maybe even a passing comment erupted into World War III. We'd find ourselves so angry at each other we'd go our separate ways and we wouldn't interact with one another sometimes for days. Keith had decided there would be no peace in the house until I initiated making up and I resolved that I would not be the first to give in. Yet when we were done we had no idea what we were arguing about in the first place. We were wasting precious energy holding on to anger. It was exhausting. Living like this can eventually take a toll on your spirit and be hard for your soul. It's awful for your relationship. Anger only causes you to be imprisoned and prevents you from feeling real joy not only in your marriage, but in any part of your life. Rather than quarreling, believers should gently instruct one another hoping that God will lead them to knowledge of truth. When you're wrong, admit it but whenever you're right, be quiet.

Conflict is a necessary part of marriage. Agreeing to disagree leads to respect and mutual admiration. The key to healthy conflict is remembering at all times you are a child of the King and you should behave according to the family code of conduct set forth in Scripture. Get rid of bitterness and rage, brawling and slander, along with every form of malice. *Be kind and compassionate to one another, forgiving each other, just as Christ forgave you. Ephesians 4:30-32*

Philippians 2:3-4 Do nothing out of selfish ambition or vain conceit, but in humility consider others better than you.

Each of you should look not only to your own interests, but also to the interests of others. Marriage should not revolve around your spouse and what they can do for you. Instead it should be centered on how you can minister to your spouse. I have been surprised by how the intense desire to help and, yes serve my husband has transformed my marriage and made the love even more powerful. I wait each evening for him to come home before I have dinner not because I'm not starving but because I want to do it for him. I go to church each Sunday that his choir sings and sit in the pews not because I wouldn't like to go to one of our other three services, but because I believe our worshipping together is important. Serving him in the small mundane routines of life is actually an expression of love. I've heard it said many times that it is the little things that can destroy a marriage and send it spiraling out of control to divorce court. I am then not surprised that all the little things make a difference.

So what should you expect from marriage? That it will be the union of two imperfect people coming together mind, body, and soul. These independent people will share a name, a checkbook, and a bed but that won't make the marriage. Expect that you will leave your old life and enter into an exclusive interdependent lifelong commitment to each other. Anticipate that your spouse will learn to respect the image of God in you and that they will never forget to pray for you daily. Never go to bed angry, (Still working on this one occasionally). Most importantly expect that each of you will be faithful to your vow. Your marriage is sacred ground. God has sanctioned it you must be determined as we are to come together for God's purposes, no longer two but one. My favorite saying is "Me and you against the world Baby." The Word tells us *"Love is not self seeking, it's not easily angered, and it keeps no record of wrong." 1 Corinthians 13:5.*

Work at growing your love and your relationship to a deeper level. Put love for God first. Make every effort to have your goals and aspirations mature as your character deepens. These are the expectations that will be rewarded.

Here are some things to remember as you embark upon your journey to marital purpose.

Marriage is a lifelong commitment. Your marriage will go through tough times, but remember you're in it for the long haul. "So they are no longer two, but one. Therefore what God has jointed together, let man not separate." "Why then," they asked, "did Moses command that a man give his wife a certificate of divorce and send her away?" Jesus replied, "Moses permitted you to divorce your wives because your hearts were hard. But it was not this way from the beginning." - Matthew 19:6-8. Don't succumb to the microwave mentality of our time. Marriage is hard work and each partner should be willing to put in their fare share to make it last. Anything worth having is worth working for. Marriage is no exception. *"Consider it pure joy, my brothers, whenever you face trials of many kinds, because you know that the testing of your faith develops perseverance." - James 1:2.*

Forgiveness is an essential expectation of marriage but it comes with a counterpart and that's forgetting.. *"For if you forgive men when they sin against you, your heavenly Father will also forgive you. But if you do not forgive men their sins, you Father will not forgive your sins." - Matthew 6:14-15.* This is a commandment with a promise. If you desire forgiveness from God you must learn to forgive. That includes your husband. But it's forgetting in marriage that can be downright impossible. How can you be expected to forget the horrible words, the devastating arguments, or worse yet, the affair? Truthfully, there is no cut and dry answer to this question. Only God can give the courage and strength to truly forgive from your heart. But it is important to remember that when you don't forgive the only person you are hurting is yourself.

Admitting when you're wrong and seeking reconciliation with your spouse can be both difficult and humbling. Many of us would rather jump off a bridge than to admit the error of our ways. But the Word says *"Therefore, if you are offering your gift at the altar and there remember that your brother has something against you; leave your gift there in front of the altar. First go and be reconciled to your brother; then come and offer your gift." - Matthew 5:23-24.* Admitting that I'm wrong has sometimes been difficult for me because in my mind it was admitting that I was imperfect, I was weak, frail. Over the years God has convicting my spirit and taught me that without Him I am weak, frail, and imperfect. Only He can perfect our imperfection. So learn to admit when you're wrong and ask for forgiveness from the one whom you've offended.

Communication, as Keith has taught me, is very important. But communication should be done from a non-judgmental, non-condemning standpoint.

Don't try to change your spouse. Instead, try to encourage and strengthen each other. You can't change your spouse, but you can change yourself.

"Why do you look at the speck of sawdust in your brother's eye and pay no attention to the plank in your own eye? How can you say to your brother, `Brother, let me take the speck out of your eye,' when you yourself fail to see the plank in your own eye? You hypocrite, first take the plank out of your eye, and then you will see clearly to remove the speck from your brother's eye. - Luke 6:41-42.

I spent years learning this lesson. Why I thought I was powerful enough to change God's creation is beyond me, but I tried to no avail. Then one day I decided that my spouse wasn't the one that needed changing. It was me. What an "aha" moment. Once I came to that realization, life was much sweeter. You do your job and allow God to do his.

Don't depend on your spouse to fill all your needs. Only God can do that.

"Cursed is the one who trusts in man, depends on flesh for his strength whose heart turns away from the LORD." - Jeremiah 17:5.

Husbands be willing to fill your God-given role. *"Husbands, love your wives, just as Christ loved the church and gave himself up for her to make her holy, cleansing her by the washing with water through the word, and to present her to himself as a radiant church, without stain or wrinkle or any other blemish, but holy and blameless. In this same way, husbands ought to love their wives as their own bodies. He who loves his wife loves himself." - Ephesians 5:25-28*

Wives be willing to fill your God-given role. *"Wives, submit to your husbands as to the Lord. 23 For the husband is the head of the wife as Christ is the head of the church, his body, of which he is the Savior. 24 Now as the church submits to Christ, so also wives should submit to their husbands in everything." - Ephesians 5:22-24*

Expect from your marriage what God expects and in the end it will lead you to a marriage of purpose.

Family of Origin

When I met Keith's parents to say I was afraid would be an understatement. My biggest fear was they would judge me for being young, divorced and with two children. In any case I went for it with all the confidence I could muster as was my usual attack mode for scary situations.

Keith's Mom and Dad were nice enough. They extended all of the usual formalities provided someone visiting their home. But there style was a little different than what I was used to. It took me a while become accustomed to their open house mentality. You see the way I grew up people didn't just show up knocking on your door. They were to call and announce themselves. There was no such thing as an unexpected visitor. More conservative in this area I marveled at the liberality taken by their friends and family. In fact I came to love it and adopt it as my own. Yep as far as I could tell we had very similar backgrounds. Nothing out of the ordinary, nothing screaming run away as fast as you can.

Keith's experience was a little different. I had managed to put the fear of God in him about my family. Their more conservative demeanor only managed to strengthen my argument. But truthfully they weren't as bad as I made them out to be. I just thought a little fear would keep him on the straight and narrow. Bad I know, but it felt right at the time.

Our similarities were many. We were both the older of two children, we had modest middle class upbringings, and religion played a role in both of our lives. The only major difference looking from the outside in, was that Keith's parents had been married to one another for many years. My parents were divorced and remarried.

Marital status aside things were looking up in the compatibility department. But sometimes it's the little things that mean a lot.

Seeing life from a different perspective, each other's perspective was hard. Trying to understand that different wasn't necessarily wrong took years for my husband and me to learn. We viewed life from two different vantage points. I was obtuse, and he was a right angle. We argued about just about everything. The usual conflict evolved around money, sex, children, and communication. At this point we weren't even mature enough to agree to disagree. My husband would become explosive and I would just shut down.

In the household I grew up in, my mother handled all the finances but in my husband's family, his father handled the finances. My sister and I were pushed to excel in academics; therefore, chores were not the number one priority. In my husband's family, academics were important but they were held to the same standard as cleaning, taking out the garbage, and mowing the yard. Each was viewed as a lesson in itself. Child rearing was an entirely different story all together. His family wielded physical discipline and mine verbal. There were times when I wished my mother would have spanked me rather than verbally scolded me, but now I understand those tongue lashings lasted far longer than any physical lashing ever could. Reconciling the two trains of thought frequently ended in a catastrophic train wreck that derailed our emotions, our thoughts, and our values. Somehow however we always managed to get back on track.

Before we were married these contrasts in our upbringing didn't seem important. Sharing a bed, a bathroom, and a bank account however turned simple differences into monumental chasms of ideology. Your money becomes your money and his money becomes his money, your children are your children and his are his. Two becoming one fades away into the mist of oblivion becoming a distant dream. But doggedly no matter what happened in our marriage, we trudged on determined like a pack of Alaskan Huskies pulling a sled uphill in a winter blizzard. We were determined to make it to the top of the mountain. Having an unhealthy relationship or getting a divorce were not options, since we both came from homes mired in both.

Understanding what you bring from your family of origin to your marriage can also help you understand one another's behaviors and attitudes more fully. This epiphany was a huge breakthrough for my husband and me.

In preparing for family life, our families of origin serve as our primary teachers. As with any other training, the quality of that education has a direct impact on our success or failure. Let's face it, many of our parents rarely role model "happily ever after" to us. For some, their marriages were merely a facade for the outside world. They may have been married for years but to what end. If the goal was simply to stay married, then motivations like financial need, religious correctness, and fear of being alone, are acceptable. However, if a healthy, happy marriage was the end result, then liking your partner and liking yourself with your partner are integral. Is the marriage of your parents a model worth following or a model worth forgetting?

Differences among a couples upbringing can cause conflict in the marriage. Hidden feelings of insecurity, abandonment and loneliness can surface at any time if not dealt with effectively. The success or failure of your marriage relationship will hinge on how well you deal with your demons. These open doors give the enemy the right to come in and take root in your marriage. Each time you argue, each time you fight unfairly, each time you reach back and pick up the seeds of these emotions you water them and help them to grow until they take root and are difficult to cut down.

I can remember many times before our epiphany, we would argue the merits of our upbringing. Determining whose family was right or wrong became the focus of our attention.

This however should not have been the objective. Instead, we should've been searching for the right prescription for our marriage; we needed to forge a plan that worked for us.

Getting in touch with feelings evolved from childhood can be difficult. No one wants to admit their parents could be wrong. Nor do they want to admit their parents weren't as happy as they seemed to be; but, Awareness will help you not to repeat the same negative patterns modeled during your formative years. Once you become aware of the patterns of your family of origin, you can change them.

Take the time to explore what you learned about life, love, and conflict in your family of origin so that you can understand how this influences your current relationship.

A couple cannot fully step into the type of marital covenant that is required by God, until they not only understand their family of origin but also apply the biblical principle of leaving and cleaving. Some men and women leave the parent physically, but are attached to them emotionally and mentally by a long rope.

This doesn't mean the parental relationship will end; it simply means it will be redefined.

Connections to family networks can be a great source of support and encouragement but was never meant to be a controlling factor in the lives of a married couple With that said, it's important to note that a common response for many married couples is to complain to their parents when the slightest of conflict arises. They are still connected, or even more connected to the family of origin than they are to their spouse. In fact, the only comments some parents hear about their son or daughter-in-law are negative ones. When allowed to continue, these comments can grow and fester in the hearts and minds of the parent leading to resentment toward the child's spouse.

I had always leaned heavily on my mother. My immediate tendency was to run to her at the smallest sign of trouble. I knew that I could always count on her to be my champion. My mother let me know early on that this was not acceptable. Her words were "Cheryl, you need to work your issues out with Keith, because you'll go back and make up with him and I'll be left hating him. I can't kiss and make up that easily." She very lovingly let me know it would be unfair to my husband to taint her perception of him.

Parents can offer great wisdom; however, we should not allow parental relations to become more important than the marital relationship. Marrying your spouse automatically moves other relationships to the secondary position.

Underlying the establishment of a proper post-marital relationship is ones ability to prayerfully and sensibly submit to this scripture.

Gen 2:24 and the man shall leave his father and mother and cleave unto his wife and the two shall become one flesh.

Grateful though you may be for the guidance and help received from parents, when one or both spouses excessively serves their family of origin and allows it to crash into their lives whenever and however it chooses it can serve as a source of conflict in the marriage. There are no boundaries to the impact this can have on the marriage. It's imperative for all concerned that the importance of building a new separate decision making unit is understood. Neither set of parents should make undue demands on the time and affections of the newlyweds.

Difficult though it was, Keith and I both learned to work within these boundaries. Each of us is the oldest and as such many times we have found ourselves catering to the needs of our families rather than the needs of one another.

I remember Keith's mom calling for him to cut her grass one day. He didn't even cut our grass. My stepfather who lives next door usually did. I was irate at the thought that he would even consider cutting someone else's grass (albeit his mother's) before he would cut his own. How dare his mother call and ask him to cut the grass when she has a husband of her own. I know, selfish but true. And don't misunderstand. I had some growing to do in this area as well. My mother's mouth was a prayer book on marriage as far as I was concerned. It took me a while to separate her reality from my own; to weed through the bitterness and discontent and use that which was good while discarding that which was destructive.

Each person in the extended family needing to know what the others are doing, or the invasion of privacy and lack of appropriately kept secrets, or one or more family members being overly controlling manifested through talking for others and telling others how to behave and feel, results in a tangling of the lives similar to finely woven fabric you can't tell where one fiber ends and the other begins. Boundaries in these families have been crossed. Maintaining privacy is an

54

integral piece of the puzzle here. The sharing of intimate needs or decisions with either set of parents should be discussed with your spouse ahead of time to avoid serious consequences in the aftermath.

Keith and I experienced a personal loss in our lives that was devastating. I chose not to share this loss with my mother because I felt it was a personal journey I needed to take on my own with my husband. Keith decided to share this intimate detail with his mother without consulting me. Imagine my surprise when she not only told my mother but came to me to express her feelings. Talk about blindsided! I was distraught. I demanded to leave immediately. I know now that neither Keith nor his mother meant any harm, but at the time I felt so violated, so dishonored. Each of them had taken it upon themselves to communicate private issues; issues that should have been kept between my husband and me without my consent, input, or permission.

Couples secure in their identities however, can give themselves to one another completely. Ultimately they can have a good relationship with their parents while combining their family backgrounds into a new and distinct entity.

Without breaking the command in Exodus 20:12 to honor your mother and your father communicate to them you love them and want to share a life with them through your actions; visiting, telephoning, and writing.

Leaving must never be interpreted as deserting. Regular contact is essential to honoring parents. Failure to communicate with parents is in effect saying "I no longer care." It's also important to honor both sets of parents equally. Remember "For God does not show favoritism." (Romans 2:11) It is necessary that the couple be equitable in visits, dinners, and vacations. In this area, Keith and I have excelled. We have managed to mesh both families together in such a way that all major family functions are enjoyed as one unit; my parents and his, his sibling and mine, our extended family, all enjoying holidays, family gatherings, birthdays, and more together.

1 Timothy 5:1 says, "Do not rebuke an older man harshly, but exhort him as if he were father."

Speaking kindly to in-laws, showing sympathy and understanding, and acknowledging their need to have continued contact with their child will go a long way in developing the in-law relationship.

Consideration must also be given to care for our own parents as they grow older. They met our physical needs when we were young. Conversely, we may have to do so as they get up in age. To fail in this responsibility is to deny our faith in Christ.

The Bible gives some beautiful examples of wholesome relationships between individuals and their in-laws; Moses and Jethro, Ruth and Naomi. Freedom and harmony are the biblical ideals for in-law relationships. The train of God's will for marriage must run on the parallel tracks of separation from parents and devotion to parents. Evaluate everyone's needs, maintain privacy, remove the chains of conformity and control. Allow yourselves to be who you are and to manifest strengths God has gifted you with.

Goals of a Successful Marriage

Fulfillment:

Spirit Emotions and Sex

I was definitely in the house physically (at least sometimes) but there were times I wasn't there emotionally. Convinced my heart was lonely I was on my own without a marital partner emotionally. I found myself despondent and disconnected. Closed off I had abandoned my husband and become uncommunicative.

He was supposed to be the love of my life.

Rooted in what was going on inside of me my unwillingness to share verbally was a manifestation of unresolved issues in the marital relationship that stimulated resentment in my spirit and resulted in my silence. Expressing this resentment through emotional detachment was my way of saying, "I don't like you, so you are a non person to me." The inner emotional reasons why I wasn't talking revolved around my trouble believing Keith genuinely loved me unconditionally. I often found myself asking does he really love me? His speech and behavior occasionally thwarted my efforts to gain significance leaving me to interpret his actions as condemnation of things I valued as being important. Once again the enemy had walked through doors I had opened. Discovering the emotions inside and the factors that gave rise to these emotions led to breaking down the wall of silence I had been living behind for so many years. That was quite the challenge but one brick at a time my Wonderful Counselor, God, helped me chisel my way through until I could see the light of day.

Asking the Holy Spirit to reveal truths to me concerning myself and my marriage led to the emotional fulfillment I was seeking. Only God had the ability to fill the emptiness I felt in my soul. Only He could validate my significance and complete me.

Then there's sex.

"I don't feel like it."

"I'm tired."

"I have a headache," common responses to Keith's advances for sex. All true. Sometimes the mere thought of having sex could make me tired and headachy. It was hard to feel like lovemaking when I was actually angry, worried, or disappointed. Understanding my need to be mentally stimulated as well as physically stimulated was like teaching a foreign language to Keith.

Arguments about sex in marriage are just about as commonplace as marriage itself. It's no secret that men and women are wired differently. I needed to feel affection and trust because the act of lovemaking was not only invasive physically but emotionally and spiritually as well. For Keith on the other hand all he needed was physical and visual stimulation. Keith thought I was passionless and I thought he was a sex fiend. No two people could've had more differing view points for the same subject.

Keith worked long hours and fatigue and stress only made matters worse. I felt neglected due to the limited amount of time we actually spent together. He would come home from work, turn on the television, sit quietly at dinner, and watch television after dinner. Then at bedtime he would become friendly—and my anger would start to sizzle on its way to a fiery inferno. Sound familiar? Telling Keith exactly what it would take to please me in bed and make me feel happy to be invited there wasn't something I was able to do at that point. I didn't know how to communicate to him my need to be courted during the day, instead of only five minutes before lovemaking. All it would take was a midday phone call, kisses on the way out the door, a long hug when he got home. But sex talk of this kind was taboo for Christians, right? I was too modest to approach the subject.

We were at an impasse he was unhappy with the quality and quantity of our sex life and I was saying, 'What's the big deal? Get a life.'" Fast becoming a major battle, I felt constantly overwhelmed and harassed about sex. Keith on the other hand felt constantly deprived, and the fights got more intense each time

Only recently has it become apparent to me that sex in marriage is a gift from God. He rejoices greatly in the intimate physical union between husband and wife, which is part of His plan for making us one. Wives can be Godly and sensual at the same time. I know hard to believe after a couple of children and about fifty pounds, but trust me "we can do all things".(hehehe) Making our intimate relationship a high priority is one of the most important things I can do for our marriage. I've spent way too much time being self conscious, self centered and a bit immature in this area. In my immaturity, I never realized how important the sexual relationship is to a man. I learned that sex is a huge need for a husband—emotionally and physically. So I've decided to be proactive rather than reactive.

Meeting my husband's needs in this regard has spilled over into every other area of our marriage. Improvement has been exponential over time. Strongholds of mistrust started coming down and lines of communication opened in ways that we never imagined possible. My husband became more tender toward me and was more responsive to my needs as well.

So as not to sound "Hollywoodish" let me tell you things didn't change overnight. I spent many hours talking to God about it. I learned from 1 Corinthians 7:3-4. "the wife's body does not belong to her alone, but also to her husband," and that the same is true for the husband. It's good for Keith to have me, and for me to have Keith.

After reading these verses I knew that I didn't have to feel guilty for not wanting to have sex or for avoiding it because Paul didn't say a wife's body belongs only to her spouse. He said her body belongs also to her spouse. As "one flesh," I share my body with Keith. Neither I nor Keith should submit to sex whenever, wherever, and however we demand it, no matter how we feel. Emphasizing mutuality and not selfishness,, since my husband's body belongs to me, I should care about it enough to give it pleasure whenever I possibly can, and he likewise with my body. In the same way, since my husband's body belongs to me, I should also be understanding and generous when I'm not necessarily "in the mood" and he likewise with my body.

Advising couples to continue to have sex on a regular basis because sex is at the heart of our sacred oneness and helps to protect our fidelity, Paul reminds us the intent of this duty isn't that a wife complies with a husband's selfish appetite for sex on demand or vice versa. Seeing sexual intimacy as a sacred responsibility rather than a duty it became more about fulfilling my sacred obligation to meet Keith's sexual needs, keep the marriage bed pure, and keep each other free of sexual temptation.

Having said this it's important to look at the husband's responsibility as well. Ephesians 5:28 says "After all, no one ever hated his own body," Paul writes, "but he feeds and cares for it, just as Christ does the church" (v.29). God describes a husband who loves his wife so much that he puts her needs at the same level of priority as his own bodily needs! In regard to sex then, if a husband loves his wife this way, there's no danger that he'll mistreat her or take sexual advantage of her, because that would be like hating his own body.

Ideally God has painted a picture of marriage with large enough brush strokes so that if a wife wasn't feeling up to sex, for whatever reason, the husband would honor and respect her feelings as if it were himself who wasn't in the mood. If a husband doesn't love his wife this way, he—not she—is sinning when he expects his wife to be available for intercourse on demand and without regard to her feelings.

Unbiblical, each of the extremes, a wife who is a slave to her husband's sexual needs and a wife who believes she has no responsibility or can shirk her obligation to nurture a healthy, ongoing sexual relationship, I recognized I had some serious soul searching to do. Regularly refusing to have sex with Keith, consistently rebuffing his sexual advances, resenting intercourse and only being willing to be intimate with him on my terms was acting selfishly. I needed to take active, positive steps toward restoring consistent and mutually satisfying lovemaking to my marriage.

Standing up for my rights may have been applauded in the world, but my marriage was not the place for it. Deciding to serve my husband, whether in bed or out, was a choice. Abstaining from sex is permissible for a period of time when we both agree to it or when it is for the purposes of prayer and fasting—but only for such times. Then we were to come back together again. Taking a "time out" from sex isn't to avoid sex—it's to pray and take active steps to bring about change. It's not to stop resentment from building; it's to bring healing so that resentment is no longer an issue. Talk about this with your husband. Tell him what you're doing and why. If he knows the goal isn't less sex, but more and better sex, he'll likely feel less threatened by a time out. Satan has an ingenious way of tempting us when we least expect it and abstinence in marriage for the wrong reasons is in his repertoire. In a world of sexual disorder it's comforting to know marriage is strong enough to contain strong sexual drives and provide for a balanced and fulfilling sexual life. A place of mutuality—our marriage bed- Keith seeks to satisfy me and I seek to satisfy him.

Another verse that changed my thinking completely was: "The man and his wife were both naked, and they felt no shame" (Genesis 2:25). I had to rid my mind of old mindsets and misconceptions and align my thoughts with God's perspective.

Needing to feel close to Keith emotionally to desire sex, I like most women wanted to spend time with him, to communicate on a deep level and feel like we were team mates in regards to housework and kids and so on. All this has to be in place for me to really desire my husband.

Keith, on the other hand, generally needed to feel close to me physically before he could invest a great deal of energy into our intimacy. I was waiting for him to be more intimate emotionally and he was waiting for me to be more tuned into him physically. That being said, it was really important for both of us to become more understanding of each other. That meant we both needed to try to imagine what it would be like to live in each other's shoes for a while. Keith was walking around feeling that if I loved him more, I would be more sensitive to his needs. Undoubtedly his feelings were those of hurt and rejection. His sexual appeal was even questioned at times.

Meeting other people's needs consumed my entire day. Whether it was caring for my children, cooking dinner, or waiting for him to come home before I ate, by the end of the day I wanted to be done need-meeting. I wanted my pillow and a remote. When I crawled into bed I wanted to go to sleep; having sex once or twice a week, with all that I did, should've been enough for him if he loved me. "He should be more responsive to the other issues in our marriage." But God convicted once more: "Are the 'needs' you meet for your husband the needs he wants met?" If dinner wasn't done would he really complain? If the kitchen floor needed mopping, he didn't say a word. And if he didn't have any socks to wear, he simply threw them in the washer himself. Realizing I regularly said "no" to the one thing he actually asked me for was an epiphany that could only have come from God. Would the world end if I didn't go to the grocery store? Unknowingly cutting my husband out of the picture, I'd become consumed with what I wanted to get done and what my children needed. Feeling bad that he never seemed satisfied, that no matter what I did, he was always unhappy didn't help matters either. Not a pleasant feeling when you love your partner.

The sex had virtually stopped as a result of my indifference. And when the sex stopped, so did the casual affection: the hand-holding, the laughing at each other's jokes, the sitting next to each other on the couch. When relationships become that icy, they risk infidelity and, ultimately, divorce. I could've chosen to say, "Why do I have to do all the work?" But contrary to popular belief the way to a man's heart is not through his stomach. The more responsive I became to Keith's needs, the more responsive he became to mine. Being the big one here I had to break the vicious circle. I didn't want my husband being resentful, angry and distant. I needed to make him feel better about our sexual relationship. Understanding the tender places in my husband's heart, I have developed compassion for him and the way he is wired.

As I have given my body as a "gift" to my husband, we have both enjoyed a very fulfilling intimate relationship that keeps getting better all the time. I also feel a deeper love for my husband than I did when we were newlyweds! Best of all, I feel that God is at the center of our marriage. I thank Him for giving us this precious gift of intimacy.

I try to remember the early part of our relationship when even though I was never highly sexed, I flirted much more. This makes a difference. I've put aside the things I've placed too much priority on, everything else I had to do and made our sexual relationship a high priority on the list. Other things can wait. Reprioritizing my time has made our marriage better. After so many years of marriage, I realized that we might need something new to renew our interest. So, I cast my inhibitions to the wind and experimented, within reason, with those things that intrigued me. As the reluctant spouse I had to make a "decision for desire." If I waited for the feeling to come over me all the time, we'd never have sex. Not showing my interest in being together sexually, Keith began to believe I had no interest in him sexually. This had to change. Still working on it, I experiment with being the initiator. As the initiator it removed some of my feelings of pressure and duty. Instead, it became something I was giving, versus something Keith was always approaching me to take. Feeling love and security I welcome this invasion as an opportunity to experience intense intimacy and pleasure with my husband.

Biblical Principles for Marriage

Marriage is a Covenant

"Keith do you take Cheryl to be your wedded wife?"
"I do."
"Cheryl do you take Keith to be your wedded
husband?"
"I do."

These were the words we spoke before God and some 200 plus witnesses on April 17, 1993. Our marriage was a covenant we made with God. But guarding it at all times has proven to be a challenge of the most formidable kind.

Unlike many couples who glide through their first few years of marriage on a cloud, Keith and I struggled. Our clouds were often filled with thunder, lightning and an occasional windstorm and even on the good days it was sunny to partly cloudy. Our differences threatened to swallow us whole and spit us back out into the cold cruel world. It was so bad at one point I kept divorce papers in the file cabinet ready to be delivered at the smallest sign of impending turmoil. I remember being so angry at Keith one time I went to the post office and mailed the divorce papers back to our house making sure he would be the one to get them from the mailbox. I know it sounds outrageous now, but it was the only way I knew to get his attention. It didn't take us long to recognize the "d" word, divorce, (I guess I can write it since I know we don't speak it) had to be banned from our relationship because leaving the door open even just a little would give us opportunity to run for the hills and never look back.. Rebuilding our desire for marriage and our desire for each other began at this point. God met us here and honored our decision.

The "d" word abolished, we accepted our promise to be in this relationship for the long haul; our success only possible if we placed God in the center and chose to find a way to not only work on but appreciate one another's differences.

Matthew 5:31-32. Jesus is trying to move us from easy divorce to a deeper commitment to marriage. The one thing that hasn't changed in our marriage is our commitment to God and the covenant we made together before Him. I may not like Keith all the time, but I am committed to love him all the time. People these days get married for the moment. They love only in the good times, only when you still look good, only when things go their way. There is no dedication to the covenant vow made on the wedding day. Keith and I chose to have a different mindset- a kingdom mindset. A mindset that says we are children of the King and come what may our ultimate goal is to look and act more like Jesus even in our marriage. We stuck it out and now we're happier than ever. We have a testimony to tell.

God's greatest commandments are to love Him and to love other people. Unconditional love for one another was a commandment. It didn't matter that we were married. We were children of God and that required love. We worship God when we love and sacrifice for our spouse. This pleases Him.

Matthew 18:20 says where even two believers are gathered in His name He will be in the midst. Because Keith and I were both believers God was already in our marriage working to transform it into a purpose driven unit. Loving real people not ideal people is the catch 22. Our marriage was a lab for learning how to love like Jesus. Testing our faith our fortitude and our resilience, each day we embarked upon a new experiment. Some days the experiment was a success, other days we had to return to our lab manual, the Bible, and formulate a new hypothesis, a new theory, that would prove our union worthy of purpose. Creating an opportunity to develop true intimacy and authenticity with another human being our marriage was the ultimate testing ground for God. He wanted each of us to go beyond the superficial. We needed to experience genuine heart to heart gut level sharing, which we still work on by the way, where Keith and I get honest about who we are and what's happening in our lives. This only happens when we open up to one another and share our hurts, reveal our feelings, confess our failures, disclose our doubts, admit our fears, acknowledge our weaknesses, and ask each other for help and prayer.

I don't always like Keith and he doesn't always like me thus the Biblical principle of discipleship can be difficult to achieve. But God will place you in situations that make it difficult to display the qualities of Christ. A marriage is no different. Truthfully there have been times when Keith and I behaved unlovely. Times when we've experienced grief brought about by the actions of the other, the upheaval of tempestuous storms, chaos, and stress, but through it all we've learned it's during those times God has taught us the true meaning of joy, patience, and peace. Our marriage has been the best work room for God to teach us to look more like Him.

Striving to reflect our ultimate service to God for which we were both made Keith and I look for ways to display our servant hood to one another and to others. Difficulties in our marriage have shaped us into effective ministers. Emerging with Godly insight because of our willingness to trust God without problems use of our spiritual gifts, passions, abilities, personalities, and experiences in counsel to others has elevated us to levels of never before seen proportions.

We have come to understand and accept that some of the very things we regret about our marriage, some of the things we wish we could forget, are the very things that God has used over and over again as we minister to and encourage couples who share the same struggles. God hasn't just used our strengths; He's used our weaknesses and even our failures to edify relationships on the brink of catastrophe.

Let's get this understood there was a point in our marriage when we both just got fed up our patience had been taken to infinity and beyond and we were getting on one another's last nerve. "God didn't care about our trivial marital issues. He couldn't or He would step in and fix it," we surmised. The love we thought we had for each other was a blur and we weren't sure if we even cared to ever feel it again. Waiting for a breakthrough was senseless and we were both tired of being hurt so we resorted in our own power to make it better. We took matters into our own hands. Feeling that in our own individuality we both were working to make things right and the other wasn't left us in uncertainty, disbelief, and despair; our hearts growing cold and our love dying. Living in a situation where we were coping rather than truly working on the problem our situation drastically drained us emotionally, physically, and spiritually. We were on life support in need of resuscitation. Our reserves were quickly being depleted and we didn't have the tools to restore our energy so we found ourselves in a crisis situation. The good news was God's power to completely turn things around hadn't gone away. Scripture tells us God never leaves us or forsakes us. This was good news for our marriage.

He's the God of miracles and restoration who makes all things new. Jesus can and did resurrect love that had died and softened our heart toward one another. He brought our marriage to life again.

Our mission as believers is to now use our marriage as a means to tell others about love. We know that if we want God to bless our marriage we have to care about what He cares about most; his lost children who need to be found. God wants everyone to know Him and His purpose for their lives. Our marriage has been a lifelong process designed to teach us to see the needs of another person as more important than our own. It's not natural, but it is a transition that must be made if we expect to enter the kingdom of heaven. Becoming this way is an intentional choice that can only be made through the power of God in each of our lives. The more we shift in that direction, the more our marriage becomes focused on the needs of others and balancing our purpose. The reward has been great.

Full of choices, life is more fulfilling when you choose to be obedient to God. It is a path to God's protection. Wisdom is a gateway to happiness. (Proverbs 3:13-20)

As you go through the various phases of marriage, it's easy to drift apart. The reasons can be many but if you are committed first to God and then to your spouse you can move through any situation.

Remember God's plan for you and your spouse are plans to prosper you and to give you a future full of hope. It is exceedingly and abundantly more than you could ever ask or think. But each of you must be willing to chase it.

The Godly Roles of Husbands and Wives

I'm buying my own home, I have a decent job, and I've been living life my way for ten years now. I'm my own woman. NO man will put me in my place. Been there, done that, bought the T-shirt and returned it. I'm an independent woman living life according to my own plan. This marriage won't define me I'm gonna define it. Submission! God must be kidding, Doesn't He know that the minute we submit to these men He put on earth they'll take advantage and walk all over us like a doormat welcoming us to "Stupidity Inn." Submission is nothing more than an invitation for misery. All I need is Jesus. He'll make my husband act right and everything will be okay.

Amazingly wonderful things can happen when you're blessed with a strong-willed personality like mine. But I hadn't matured enough to allow the Holy

Spirit to be in control of these traits that after all had kept me afloat as a single parent all these years. Serious conflicts arose as I tried to have a marriage that followed God's ordained authority structure. As a strong-willed woman, I struggled to let go of control and really allow my husband to take his God given role in our home. Learning to do this was a process and I was a reluctant student who often ignored the lessons being taught. Failure after failure with each inevitable test left me in the corner with my dunce cap on wondering why a scholar like myself had not passed each test with flying colors. Nonetheless, each time I left the corner I understood more and more the need to study, the need to learn this lessons God wanted to teach me so my marriage could be blessed by Him.

But as a woman with a will of iron I thought fast, moved fast, made decisions fast, and expected others to do the same. When Keith didn't meet my expectations in this area I stepped in and did it for him. He was willing to make more decisions but I didn't allow him the time he needed to do so. And if the decision he made wasn't the same one I would've made there was hell to pay. He became more cautious and slow in his decision making not because he wouldn't or couldn't lead but because I wouldn't allow him the freedom to do so.

Deep down inside I wanted him to lead. I really did. What woman in her right mind wouldn't want to bask in the knowledge she was covered by a man after God's own heart. One who was willing to love her unconditionally just as God does, one who would lay down his life for her just as the word of God requires. I wanted him to be the head of the household. I didn't really have the desire to seize his God- given position of leadership. I knew what the Bible said on the subject and I wanted to do what God wanted because I understood that God's ways work best. But I was afraid because I didn't want Keith to use submission as a weapon against me. I wasn't sure he had fully chosen in his heart to be fully submitted to God. I know God didn't say submit to my husband only if he proves to be worthy but I couldn't bring myself to a point of full trust in God in this area of my life mostly because of past problems and mistakes, needless to say giving Keith the wheel to my life was difficult at best. I had done it before, submitted to a male and my trust was violated, it was even more difficult for me to trust now. I wasn't at all sure I could trust him to have my best interest at heart. Could Keith really navigate the course of our lives together? I had trouble going along with his decisions when he refused to consider my thoughts, feelings, and insights on the subject. So, I fought and fought hard.

The breakthrough came and I made the choice to submit to Keith when I could discern he had made the choice to submit to the Lord. It was my sign that it was safe to submit to him. The goal here was to help me, not force me, into proper alignment.

Keith's submission to God became apparent when the way he interacted with me was in alignment with Ephesians 5:22, "Husbands, love your wives, just as Christ also loved the church and gave Himself for her" (verse 25). The way he loved me protected me, provided for me, and cared for me. He didn't neglect, ignore, demean or abuse me. He wasn't rude or disrespectful. He wasn't arrogant or insensitive. And He didn't criticize me or make me feel I wasn't valuable as he once did. To love and to cherish that's what the wedding vows say. And like most wives that's what I needed-to be cherished. So while God gives the husband a position of leadership in relationship to his wife, He also requires the price of self-sacrifice from him and that's exactly what I began to feel from Keith once he submitted himself wholly and fully to God.

You see Keith's revelation was he had been called to lead, not to control. He wasn't to use his role for selfish benefit. Instead his role of leadership was one of service. He learned not to deviate from the purpose of God's headship because if he did he would lose God's endorsement. This is the fatal mistake many husbands make when they try to brow beat their wives into submission. Totally missing the strings God has attached to their leadership role they allow their motives for leading a marriage spiritually to become mixed with selfish gain. Because Keith was allowing God to lead him, his heart was open to God and His purposes, Keith's headship received God's blessings.

Service is the foundation upon which God has given husbands the authority to lead. But like most men Keith found juggling this responsibility difficult even though he was well - meaning. Out of his own selfishness and insecurity he would at times find himself barking out orders and making demands on myself and the children rather than following the precepts and examples displayed in the Bible.

Thinking of others, especially me first, ahead of himself, was more like the picture the Bible painted of Keith's role in the marriage. At issue is our present day culture which undergirds the "me" mentality. Being a servant leader runs counter cultural to popular beliefs. Let's face it: If you're following Scripture, you're going the opposite direction on a one-way street with everyone else honking their horns at you and questioning your sanity. But God's Word tells us not to be conformed to this world but to be transformed by the renewing of our minds.

Representing Jesus in the home is Keith's primary role. Living not for himself, but as a channel of God's goodness in my life he is to respond, react, speak, and think toward me in ways that enable me to develop who I am and to develop my gifts as a way to bring glory to God. Bringing out God's glory in me and lifting me up leaves me feeling valued, special and loved. In this way Keith honors God and worships Him.

Single-minded in His mission of love as He spent time with the disciples and communicated with them, Jesus taught them about forgiveness and led by example Helping to strengthen the disciples where they were weak He defended them, praised them before others, and revealed Himself to them. In this way husbands should also love their wives.

Putting me first over children, parents, siblings, work, TV, and hobbies and learning my "love language"— the way I tend to best express and receive love from others—and packaging his love in a way that speaks to me and meets my needs has strengthened our marriage.

Knowing I was number one in Keith's life was important. If it came down to an evening with his buddies or an evening with me I needed to know He would choose me not because he had to but because he wanted to. I had an insatiable need to hear the words I love you. Hearing from him throughout the day meant the world to me. Keith may never know the effect he has on me by being gentle, tender, and making me feel cared for.

Cherishing me didn't mean sacrificing success at work or nights out with the boys. Instead when I was satisfied in knowing that I took first place in his life, when I knew I was the most important thing in the world to him I now encourage him to do the things he enjoys. Truly genuinely cherished I'm free to encourage my husband's independence. I no longer complain about nights out with the fellas because I feel secure in my position of importance.

Keith's loving me unconditionally, the same way God loves all of us helped me see more fully God's love and regard for me, and this in turn brought glory to Him.

Expecting us to care for one another God would be defiled if Keith neglected or demeaned me. Robbing me of what God wants for me Keith would in turn rob himself of growth and development. Either of us denying the personal potential of the other would cause our marriage to become dormant and thus unusable for God's purposes.

Practically speaking, Keith's sacrificial love is best displayed by volunteering to bathe the children or massage my feet, going shopping with me or taking me on a quiet walk in the park—even after he's put in a twelve-hour work day. Participating in something that is important to me demonstrates his commitment to love me sacrificially as God has instructed.

Keith's display of sacrificial love manifested itself in many ways including his dedication to praying with and for me, calling me daily just to see how I'm doing, learning to say these three phrases: "You were right," "I was wrong," and "I am sorry." (Something he does a lot better than I do, although I'm learning) and asking for and valuing my opinion. He listens to my suggestions and concerns and follows them. He has been willing to learn, change, and grow. He is appreciative of the fact that I, as a woman, am innately gifted with knowledge, insights, and abilities that he doesn't have. He is learning to understand me, how I think and how I respond emotionally. He's learning to respond to what I need to feel loved and fulfilled in our marriage. He is learning that sometimes I just need him to listen to the problem rather than fix it. Knowing that he empathizes with my pain and feels my feelings means more to me than anything. He has come to understand that lecturing instead of listening only makes matters worse. He tries to see and experience the world the way I do instead of explaining to me why I shouldn't see it that way. He shows his respect for me by not trying to change or manipulate me, but rather, honors my needs, wishes, values, and rights. He's honest with me. He doesn't hide. In return for this respect I am able to relax. I don't have a compulsive need to prove myself an equal, as I once did. He shares his hurts, his fears, his concerns, his disappointments, and his life with me. His vulnerability draws us closer than we could ever have imagined. I know he's leading in love and I don't mind following.

Now Keith's total submission to God was not something that happened over night. It didn't occur by happenstance. There were some very important things that he needed in order to take his proper place has the head of the family. As his wife I was in the best position to set the atmosphere for this transition. One of the most important lessons I learned in the process was that I needed to stop asking God to change him and instead ask God to change me and make me into the wife He had called me to be. This meant I had to stop blaming others, stop denying the behaviors, and stop avoiding responsibility for my behaviors. I had to learn how to take ownership of my part of the problems that came up in our relationship and I had to learn to apologize and seek forgiveness for them.

As I began to evolve God revealed several truths to me about what Keith needed if he was to take his rightful place as servant leader of our home. I must admit before these revelations, I never knew how important appreciation, autonomy, and recreation were to a man. I was totally in the dark.

For me appreciation meant validation but for Keith it meant achievement. He as a man, needed to have his achievements recognized no matter how big or how small.

I distinctly remember one particular argument about paying bills. I believe my final response was "Paying bills is what you're suppose to do. If you don't help pay bills do you think I'll be in the dark by myself?"

The problem was Keith needed me to recognize his achievements and show appreciation for what he was doing to maintain our household. It didn't matter whether or not he was doing it alone. This notion went completely over my head. In that one sentence I had managed to totally undermine his self worth. Not my intention but still damaging to his personal power. Continuing in this mode would lead to his losing the motivation to try. He would feel inadequate and incapable of giving support.

Keith's need for autonomy was the one I understood the least. While I could be in his presence all day, as a man, he needed time to be alone to mull over his problems and solve them if possible.

When under pressure, Keith, like most men, needed some space. He didn't want to talk about the problem. He became aloof, preoccupied, and unresponsive; getting his attention at these times is futile. Instinctively I wanted to support him but he needed time to regroup and I have learned to give him that time.

Recreation time was much easier. It wasn't very hard to identify those things he enjoyed doing and find a way to fit in. My idea of intimacy was sharing with one another and talking things out but he connected by doing things together, so, football Sunday it is. Being his recreational companion turned out to be enjoyable, tailgating, football Sunday at the house. We discovered we weren't only husband and wife, we were friends.

Everything I've said so far brings us to my point on submission. A two way street designed by God as a lifestyle for all Christians, I needed to uproot some old ideas before I could plant new ones.

Overemphasis on submission to husbands and under emphasis on submission to God caused me to see submission as a place of inferiority and lack of fulfillment. This coupled with some husbands need to resort to physical and verbal abuse as they demanded submission from their wives made the whole idea lose its appeal in my book. Truthfully submission is a choice we make in our hearts. Voluntarily placing yourself under the will of God exemplifies the origins of true submission. Ephesians 5:21 says we are to submit to one another out of reverence for Christ. Responsibility for submission rests with each of us. Submission is the most integral piece of the puzzle when declaring to be a Christian. Your attitude should be the same as that of Christ the ultimate submitter.

Too often people confuse "submit" with "obey." The Bible gives commands about obeying other people but only in regard to children and slaves, and in the context of the local church. (Ephesians 6:1, Ephesians 6:5, Hebrews 13:17). Being neither Keith's child nor his servant the word "obey" had no application to our relationship as husband and wife. Therefore Keith demanding submission of me would've only become intimidating and oppressive, which would then breed resentment. Keith understood using submission as a tool to hurt and destroy me or being more interested in my submission to him than in his own submission to God would send us into a tailspin we might not ever recover from.

Submitting to God doesn't suppress us but rather frees us to become who we're made to be, within the boundaries of His protection. In the same way my submitting to Keith comes under his covering and protection, and this frees me to become all God created me to be.

Ultimately the goal of a stronger and more intimate marital relationship is the plan of Biblical submission. To bless us and enrich our lives god requires us to be in submission. Opening your heart to understand submission from God's point of view and practice it in love will help you to trust Him and realize He will not require anything of you that is not for your good and blessing.

After You Say I Do

Holy Matri-Money

What's yours is mine and what's mine is mine. My husband and I tease one another about this all the time. Well meaning women including those closest to me have often advised me to make sure I had my own stash because there could come a time when I would need it. What happened to two becoming one?

Mark 10:21 And Jesus, looking upon him, loved him, and He said to him, You lack one thing; go and sell all you have and give to the poor, and you will have treasure in heaven; and come accompany Me.

What does money mean to you? Do you hoard money or are you too generous? Do you gravitate toward financial tasks or do you avoid them altogether?

Does it make you feel powerful, anxious, guilty, loved, responsible or secure? What assumptions and values about money did you develop while you were growing up? Mind-sets about money deeply ingrained and embedded into your psyche can make it difficult to transverse the financial mountain in marriage.

Differing money personalities, a lack of financial savvy, and little or no communication in this area caused Keith and I to face a serious marital crisis. Our deepest needs, masked by money issues, collided and paralyzed us from making progress into a healthier, happier marriage. Even now it occasionally rears its ugly head. We didn't know how to financially forge a new identity as a married couple without forfeiting our individual identities. In my family my mother handled the finances. In his it was his father. Our arguments grew not from fear that we couldn't afford specific purchases, but from fear we couldn't afford to give in to each other's spending preferences. Understanding how our concepts of money were shaped by the families we grew up in helped us tremendously. We both came from families that viewed money as a symbol of success and autonomy. But now that we were married, spending what we wanted, when we wanted, was creating a tug-of-war; each of us flailing in the mud with no hope for rescue. Our individual financial styles felt right because it reflected attitudes and values that were familiar. Moving from individual to shared control of finances was threatening because we were still learning to trust one another in other areas of life. No matter how open we'd become, money continued to be treated with evasiveness because it was concrete and quantifiable. It became the focus of conflicts that were really about something more intangible. For instance each of us was afraid of the other's perceived power, but we agreed that neither of us wanted to hold it over the other.

As we moved into our middle years we both still felt an uncomfortable tension brewing over money, the disagreements multiplied as our responsibilities mounted: "Who gets what? How much? When? And how are we going to manage it?" We brought in plenty of money. But when it was time to pay the bills, we always struggled.

To the casual observer we appeared to be making wise financial choices. We weren't in credit card debt and we weren't living an extravagant lifestyle, but it never occurred to either of us that we were overspending. We made good money we just didn't understand what happened to all of it."

Keith and I felt stretched to the limit and saw few good options that would improve our situation. Keith felt the weight of responsibility for providing and I know he envied me sometimes because not only did I get more time with the kids, I didn't have the burden of everyone's financial well-being depending on my income.

I couldn't help but notice Keith's fatigue and frustration. It concerned me that he worried so much about money, and I always wondered if I should increase my hours at work. But then I wondered if Keith, even though he was the one who told me to decrease them, would view my working longer hours as a lack of confidence in his ability to provide. Would the increase in my income be worth the additional time spent away from home?

Not knowing the answers, I settled for trying to cut spending, but still felt I was to blame for the financial pressures. Keith's role as primary provider was so clear-cut; he didn't have to figure out how to divide up his life—and end up feeling guilty no matter what decision he made.

We were actually making our struggle more difficult because we hadn't shared with one another our thoughts and worries. We had unwittingly allowed our financial pressures to create distance between us. Reluctance to share our concerns openly put us at risk of becoming resentful.

So then how did we begin to rectify a bad financial situation; by gaining a biblical understanding of money. *"A man's life does not consist in the abundance of his possessions" (Luke 12:15).*

Believing most of our problems would be solved if we had more money many of us spend our lives chasing the illusion. The reality is more money can also complicate your life. How often have we heard millionaires committing suicide obviously because they weren't happy? Meaningful lives are not found in money. Instead they're found in our relationships—first with God, then with our spouse and family, and finally with others. Decisions influenced by money are usually poor ones.

Matthew 6:19-24 do not gather and heap up and store up for yourselves treasures on earth, where moth and rust and worm consume and destroy, and where thieves break through and steal. But gather and heap up and store for yourselves treasures in heaven, where neither moth nor rust nor worm consume and destroy, and where thieves do not break through and steal; for where your treasure is, there will your heart be also. The eye is the lamp of the body. So if your eye is sound, your entire body will be full of light. But if your eye is unsound, your whole body will be full of darkness. If then the very light in you [your conscience] is darkened, how dense is that darkness! No one can serve two masters; for either he will hate the one and love the other, or he will stand by and be devoted to the one and despise and be against the other. You cannot serve God and mammon (deceitful riches, money, possessions, or whatever is trusted in).

Living in a materialistic society has spawned the practice of loving money and using people rather than using money and loving people. All their lives spent collecting and storing only to die and leave it behind these people live lives with an empty existence that depletes their very souls. Neglecting the essence of what life is truly about they create a façade that when looked at more closely deteriorates under the inspection. Integrity, character, and accountability are all lost behind the fake reality. Everything else takes a back seat. Their desire for money and what it can buy far outweighs their commitment to God and spiritual matters. Whatever you store up you will spend much time thinking about. Don't fall into the materialistic trap because the love of money is the root of all evil. (1Timothy 6:10). Can you honestly say God and not money is your master?

I believe in giving. But it's important that you maintain a balance even in your giving. Proverbs 6:1-5 My son, if you have become security for your neighbor, if you have given your pledge for a stranger or another, You are snared with the words of your lips, you are caught by the speech of your mouth. Do this now my son, and deliver yourself when you have put yourself into the power of your neighbor; go, bestir and humble yourself, and beg your neighbor. Give not sleep to your eyes, nor slumber to your eyelids; Deliver yourself, as a roe or gazelle from the hand of the hunter, and as a bird from the hand of the fowler.

Not a plea against generosity but against overextending one's financial resources and acting irresponsibly in ways that could lead to poverty this verse reminds us of the importance of maintaining balance between generosity and good stewardship. I have heard stories of people sowing into what they perceived to be good ground only to find out they had been deceived. As with anything you must seek God and ask for His direction when giving.

Luke 12:33 Sell what you possess and give donations to the poor; provide yourselves with purses and handbags that do not grow old, an unfailing and inexhaustible treasure in the heavens, where no thief comes near and no moth destroys. For where your treasure is, there will your heart be also.

The key to using money wisely is to see how much we can use for God's purposes, not how much we can accumulate for ourselves. If your financial goals and possessions hinder you from giving generously, loving others, or serving God bring your thoughts into perspective. If you concentrate your money in your business your thoughts will center on making the business profitable. If you direct it toward other people you will become concerned with their welfare.

Money was designed to be our servant, never our master. It's to be used to build our marriage and family and to honor God. Getting a proper perspective on money is the first step to solving financial conflicts.

Coming to the conclusion that we must embrace our God given differences, even about money, because God had designed and placed different gifts and abilities into our marriage to provide balance we are seeking God's help as we develop a healthy money personality-even if it means He must show us where our attitudes have been unhealthy or sinful. We have made ourselves available to take the right steps toward healing and fiscal wisdom. We don't label our attitudes as right or wrong. We try to understand one another's money history listening for hurts, fears, wishes, and hopes that could be funneled into money matters. Trying to empathize rather than criticize we honor each other's needs so we can respectfully negotiate financial decisions because we understand respect breeds trust

I have had to become a truth teller in this area. Remember, some very well meaning women whom I trusted implicitly said to always keep a stash. So, I remember when I would go out and get credit cards, unknown to Keith, for the purpose of having funds at my disposal. Wrong! This proved to be disastrous.

We are still working on keeping track of how much money we have, and making sure the important things—such as bills—are paid first. By weighing our current expenses against our future goals, we have the freedom to go out to dinner now and then, or even take a vacation, knowing we can actually afford to do it. By temporarily suspending our own beliefs and seeing what we could teach each other we have stretched ourselves to a place of mutual satisfaction

Handling our finances is no longer a job to do alone we do it together. It is so much easier if we work as a team. Learning to verbalize our feelings we are much better equipped now to find mutually satisfying solutions when we do clash over finances.

Living within our means gives us peace of mind. Instead of creating tension, our finances now unite us in our common goals of spending wisely, giving generously, and saving for our future.

Listing priorities helps us discover what is valuable. Identifying top priorities we share and what it means for our budget moves us closer to congruency and enjoyment of things like family holidays.

God's been so faithful to us. We certainly have repercussions from our years of financial mismanagement, but we didn't have to declare bankruptcy or head to divorce court. Even at our worst point, we discovered God's blessings never stop. What's the meaning you assign to money?

Forgive and Forget

Shortly after Keith and I were engaged I found out something that threatened to tear us apart forever. He had a child; one I knew nothing about for over a year. How was I supposed to deal with that? To make matters worse everyone knew about it except for me. Here I was anxious and concerned I would be tying him down with two sons and here he had a daughter. My anger and hurt weren't about the child, but about the betrayal and the anguish he allowed me to drown in because of my own two children. Could my Christian background help me to forgive or would I revert back into the cynical unforgiving person I once was, believing all men were dogs and none of them deserved a woman like me.

We've heard it before "Forgive and forget." But if we could forget, we wouldn't need to forgive. Rather, when our injuries are great, we need to go through the process of forgiveness. But believe me the process isn't easy because its at this point you've made the choice to turn away from your spouses poor choices. You must also give up your right to punish.. It's ultimately a choice not one based in feelings and emotions because if we waited on our feelings we would never forgive.

Keith and I are like every other couple in the world. We have said and done things to hurt, distress, and demean one another. Yet, through it all we have managed to rely on one thing; forgiveness. We have learned to be committed to forgiveness. We seek to process our hurt without condemnation. Refusing to let go of grudges or give up score keeping. only caused us to replay our grievances over and over. We were so busy rehashing and trying to be right that .only our negative thoughts dominated our thinking. Now we're honest about the pain caused because it's a consequence of our poor choices but we don't throw it in one another's face or use it as a weapon since we want to rebuild the relationship, not tear it down. At first I went too far the other way, trying to hide the pain because I didn't want to argue or fight. Then I realized this was unhealthy for both of us. We each needed to know how the other was feeling, when we handled it without being defensive, we both moved forward in rebuilding trust. Ultimately we had to release old mind sets that said forgiveness: dismisses the offender's moral responsibility or that it's forgetting the offense, or a once-for-all event. Instead we had to replace these mindsets with ones that affirmed forgiveness as a choice as being willing (when appropriate) to allow the offender to rebuild responsible trust and an exercise of disciplinary measures with redemptive intent being willing to work toward reconciliation.

A marriage can't survive without the spirit of forgiveness. This is one of the most important elements of any relationship. Not forgiving opens the door for the enemy to work in your life. You see just as we can open the door for God's spirit to come in and fill us and elevate us to a higher level of operating in Him there are also doors we can open to allow Satan's intervention in our lives. Bringing in levels of demonic strongholds and hindrances anger not properly dealt with can become such a door. The enemy thrives on bitterness and un-forgiveness, and it's a wide open door for them to move right in on a person and develop many spiritual, mental and even physical bondages. Un-forgiveness not only gives demons the right or ability to torment us, but it also prevents God from forgiving our own sins! Now this is serious, this means that when we cry out for God's help, but have un-forgiveness in our hearts, He looks down and our sins are before Him. It puts up a wall in our relationship with our heavenly Father. Jesus was very clear that if we are to be forgiven, we cannot be unforgiving towards others.

Beyond this, bitterness is also a very common means for a born again believer to become spiritually defiled, that is, polluted or unclean spiritually. (Hebrews 12:15) So then how do we move through the process of forgiveness? The first step is to pray and acknowledge to God that you have become angry. Many of God's people need help, but can never get the help they need because they simply won't acknowledge their need of God's help and deliverance. Before we can get any kind of deliverance from God, we must first acknowledge our condition, and the fact that we need God's help.

The Second step of forgiveness is to pray for forgiveness of your spouse. This step is often times very difficult for us because usually we don't feel like praying for our spouse when they have hurt us but our prayer life should not be based upon how we feel, but rather, on an act of our will. We must be disciplined in prayer to pray for the things that we need to pray for rather than praying for the things that we feel like praying for. When anger comes upon us, we must pray out of discipline rather than feelings – asking for forgiveness for our spouse in spite of.

Praying for forgiveness for someone who offended us should be done simply out of obedience. It went against every feeling that I had in my heart sometimes to pray for Keith but God gently reminded me that He forgives me on a daily basis for sins that are far more grievous to Him than anything that Keith could ever do.

He reminded me that He not only forgave me, but He paid for my sins in the ultimately act of love: He gave His life. Eventually I realized the more I continued to pray for Keith, it changed from being a prayer of words from my head to actually meaning what I said from my heart. In the end forgiveness was the only thing that uprooted and closed the door to the spirit of anger and its manifestations.

Forgiveness changes us not our spouse.

Can We Talk?

Dressed in a fetching black jumpsuit, I was prepared for an evening of a lifetime to commemorate my 30th birthday. Visions of family and friends, good food, and good music danced in my head as I intuitively suspected my husband of whisking me away to a surprise party he had planned.

Married for three years, I was sure my husband had learned hospitality 101 from me by now. I was the "Party Diva" Every special occasion from birthdays to promotions was a reason to celebrate and I threw some great ones. From luaus to fiestas, you name it I'd done it. You never knew what to expect when you came to a Donovan party. But, much to my dismay, this party bug had not yet infected my husband. In fact he hadn't even developed a fever. How could he not notice all the love and thought I put into each of my grand productions? Down to the last detail. Even the toothpicks in the fruit matched the theme of the event. Identifying the likes and dislikes of the honoree, I always tried to make each gala special by incorporating something special into their day; surprise guests, specially planned meals, all orchestrated to perfection. Now it was my turn.

Traveling the brightly lit roads to our destination devilish thoughts entered my mind. My horns appeared as I heard the voice inside my head say' "This isn't the way to the Roof my favorite R&B club. How could he not be taking me there? He knows how much I love it and how much fun we have there. Well, all I know is, if he isn't taking me to the Roof, he must've found something better. After all I only turn 30 once."

Pulling into the parking lot of a club I didn't recognize, my thoughts exploded like a time bomb in my head. "Where are we? What kind of place is this? Why did he bring me here?"

I still had high hopes for the evening, but those hopes were soon shattered into tiny pieces like glass from a fragile crystal vase full of delicate flowers left unattended by their owner. At this point I wanted to pick up those pieces and cut somebody. My attitude had gone from "kid in the candy store" happy to "woman scorned" evil in a matter of seconds.

The club was loud and brazen, not anything I was accustomed to. The guest list was admirable, but with invitations going out only two days before the event everyone had other plans. The refreshments were okay, but what's this, my name is misspelled on the cake.

"Oh my God, we've been married for three years and he doesn't even know how to spell my name! Could he have put any less thought into this? Think of me any less? He could've taken me to Whataburger and bought my favorite Whatameal™ and I would feel more special than I do right now! At least it would've required some thought about what I like!"

The honeymoon phase: laughter, love and excitement everyday was over. Reality hit us like a ton of bricks causing us to swell to hideous proportions under the compromise, conflict resentment and deepening frustration that was our marriage.

But wait a minute, had I ever really articulated my wishes to him, my likes, and my dislikes? No, like most women, I expected he would instinctively discern my needs. I wanted him to read my mind. I had broken all the rules of communication. Not having added the proper ingredients for one on one discussion, I was now boiling over like a pot of steaming water. The predictable conflict would end as it always did with blaming, yelling, and withdrawing.. Just like other couples, I was a woman and he was a man and we communicated and received information differently.

Disagreements were literally unavoidable: finances, sex, priorities, in-laws, and parenting, take your pick each could be selected from the menu as the argument of the day. Sometimes you could get two for one.

I was operating from a preconceived idea that somehow by osmosis, my husband would pick up my penchant for hospitality. The party however was just another piece in a long chain of surface issue arguments that really stemmed from a lack of true discourse. We were disconnected because we didn't really know how to talk to one another about what was going on in our lives. We were unsure about how to get our points across or how to express ourselves. Eager to say what was on our mind, we rarely took the time to listen. Our comeback was formulated before the other person could finish the sentence. Proverbs 18:13 He who answers before listening that is his folly and his shame "You always" and "I never" were consistent elements of our repertoire: Poor word choices of course because they were too vague and caused us to tune one another out. Both worthy opponents in the blame game, we both knew it took one person to start the argument, but neither of us, with our winner take all attitudes, wanted to take responsibility for our contributions.

Rehashing the past became a science for me as I craftily mixed one part reality with one part emotion and came up with a volatile concoction aimed at destroying my husband's fortitude for standing up under the pressure of his past mistakes. Sarcasm and mocking became my weapons of choice. In an attempt to get him before he got me, I used these weapons like a knife going for the jugular every time. Neither of us really thought about our words and how devastating they could be to the other person until well after the squabble was over; our war of words had as its spoils hurt emotions, weakened spirits, and disillusioned minds. These destructive patterns of disagreement from the past left behind emotional scars that were difficult to heal

Struggling often to put my feelings into words after an emotional battle, I would withdraw and shut my husband out with silence just to avoid conflict. Submerging my differences of opinion instead of dealing with them honestly I tried to sidestep the argument because it was painful. I didn't feel free to discuss frustrations and disagreements with my husband because I didn't like the outburst it produced. I held back because keeping peace with Keith kept him in a good mood. I had always resisted discussing problems it often left me empty an exercise in futility because efforts to resolve our differences ended in silence or shouting matches, experiences I didn't care to repeat. So, I'd just sit in my little stew of resentment trying not to raise any sensitive subjects, fearing the resulting argument would degenerate into a verbal battle.

Stemming from feelings of being overwhelmed, threatened, provoked, criticized, or just misunderstood, there were other times I would let go with the force of a charging herd of elephants not caring who was in my path. This out of control self expression can only be likened to the fool mentioned in Proverbs 29:11.

Feelings buried so as not to provoke Keith only stayed buried for the short term. They eventually came to a head. I remembered situations much longer than Keith did, but I made sure to remind him during these tirades. My passive aggressive behavior of nagging and blaming was just as dangerous to our marriage as Keith's more aggressive behavior. On many nights this led to my lying as far on my side of the bed as I could and Keith would do the same. I'd be thinking about the terrible things Keith said to me spending most of the night unable to fall asleep. Keith on the other hand, exhausted from the raging anger he displayed and thinking about how unreasonable I had been drifted off to sleep. We had developed a habit of allowing our arguments to get out of control. Not resolving the problem gave us an initial feeling of peace and harmony, but it was like a wound that heals on the surface when underneath there's an infection that needs to be released. No one enjoys lancing the wound, but real recovery can't take place otherwise. Keith was left with no choice but to assume what was wrong and draw his own conclusions. 99% of the time he was wrong and this only made matters worse as the frustration and negative feelings built up like an old pressure cooker inside me exploded in an uncontrollable fit of venomous verbal assaults because of his inability to figure it out.

Confronted once more with learned behaviors for dealing with marital conflict we had to reframe our thinking, realign the way we handled disagreements to better reflect the pattern God wanted to see. Instead of justifying our behavior we learned how to properly react to disagreements no matter how intense they were or who was at fault. We learned to see through conflict and search for the real issues that were submerged under the surface of our shallow pool of volatile emotions. Bringing God into the conversation didn't hurt. His wisdom always helped when we couldn't find the answer on our own. Looking for mutually beneficial solutions and resolutions and calling a time out when one of us was too emotionally charged to continue diffused the situation and led us to calmer more quiet discussions. Each time we worked out a disagreement this way we were better equipped to deal with the next one. It fine-tuned our relationship:

Then there were the times we couldn't agree. No matter how much we tried we could not come to a mutually satisfying conclusion. Each of us wanted to win the battle and be right. For me conclusion was everything. But we've learned over the years every difference of opinion doesn't have to be settled. We no longer expect to agree on everything. Remembering that our relationship, not the issue, is the most important thing we often ask ourselves if our motives for the disagreement are selfish. If they are we pray about our differences and let them go. After all it was our differences that attracted us to one another in the first place. Just because we had differing opinions didn't mean we weren't compatible or that we were drifting apart. We became willing to not get defensive nor to insist on winning at all costs. Agreeing to disagree helped us to appreciate one another's uniqueness.

Developing and strengthening our relationship was the only refuge for our vacillating marriage: Proverbs 27:17 "As iron sharpens iron, so one man sharpens another." The iron we were sharpening was cutting away at our marriage rather than strengthening it. Taking the first step, Keith suggested counseling.

Revelation upon revelation came pouring out when we recognized communication as a primary function of marriage. Phil 2:1-4 If you have any encouragement from being united with Christ, if any comfort from his love, if any fellowship with the Spirit, if any tenderness and compassion, then make my joy complete by being like-minded, having the same love, being one in spirit and purpose. Do nothing out of selfish ambition or vain conceit, but in humility consider others better than yourselves. Each of you should look not only to your own interests, but also to the interests of others. Personal development in the areas of self discipline

Proverbs 25:28 Like a city whose walls are broken down is a man who lacks self-control and objectivity soon followed.

Focusing on my way as the right way (and sometimes the only way) when people did things differently I felt the need to correct them. But learning to control our tongue will make a huge difference in our relationship with our husbands. The key to this step is to learn to accept your husband's differences and to understand that different does NOT mean wrong. If you continue to criticize your husband or redo what he's done, you undermine your attempts to let him lead.

The other side of controlling your tongue is learning to give praise on a regular basis. You need to learn to look for the good in this man that God has blessed you with, and be open with your praise. Make a conscious effort to look for things that he does or traits that you see in him that are praiseworthy and shower him with these comments. Say things that let him know that you trust and respect him and his ability to lead your household. These statements will make him start to feel like the man of the house again and like the man God created him to be.

Train up a Child

Parenting is an awesome responsibility. God has chosen us to be stewards over his most precious creation: mankind. Parenting can be the most rewarding and most devastating responsibility all at the same time. You will experience triumphs and failures, mountains and valleys, highs and lows. But the bottom line is we must constantly seek God's face and follow His examples as we parent our children. Why, because like us as children of God, our children will make mistakes, disappoint us, and do the opposite of what we have trained them to do, but like God, as parents we must continue to love them unconditionally and show them grace and mercy even when they fall Parenting is something you do and not just who you are.

Let's face it: children can be hard on a marriage especially in a blended family. Parenting is usually much more work than we bargained for especially when you realize that you are responsible for the welfare and moral development of a living, breathing human being forever. Whether the child lives with you or not it can bring discord to the marriage if you let it. Add to the equation two differing schools of thought on child rearing and you're an accident waiting to happen.

"You're too soft on em."

"Well you're too hard."

"You let em do what they want."

"Well you don't let em do anything."

"You don't see what they're doing."

"Well you only see the bad."

Time out has anyone consulted the manual? If not then we're all wrong! Thank God He doesn't love His children the way we sometimes love ours! Using the Word of God to rear your children is the only way to go. Now that doesn't mean they'll turn out perfect but it does mean they will have a firm foundation on which to stand. Seek the Word of God for His will in your children's lives and stand on it. Use His example as you discipline, guide and nurture your children. Remember that He is not overbearing, impatient, and double minded. Instead He is loving, patient, and kind. He's not quick to throw in the towel but instead He forgives over and over and over again and He's always there with open arms waiting to accept us back into the fold. Your children are your greatest legacy and you are their greatest protector. God has bestowed you with the heavy responsibility of nurturing another person's soul. Don't take that responsibility lightly. Children will notice when your faith isn't consistent with the precepts you have been teaching. So, be an example of faith before your child. Let them hear and see you praying and the Word of God. Give them praise reports about how God has delivered you and created open doors in your life. Mere references to faith are not enough. Your relationship with God should be woven into the fabric of your life. We are instructed to bring our children up in the "nurture and admonition of the Lord." Don't be afraid to walk the walk and talk the talk. The results will bless you. Don't stop parenting too soon. Many parents make this mistake by assuming once their children reach a certain age they no longer need a parent. On the contrary this is the point in their lives when they need you most especially the teen and early adult years. You see when they were young, they needed you to provide for them and protect them. Now they need you to mentor them.

Let them know you're still concerned about where they go and who they see. My mother always calls it a square one. I'm in my forty's, married, with two grown children of my own and I still call my mother and let her know when I'm leaving out of town or going to a strange place. Be proactive and even aggressive if necessary.

Delicately balancing challenging them to do better with tough love without demeaning them eliminates the threat of provocation. We must challenge our children to succeed. Love your children for who they are, just as they are. Contrary to popular opinion, you cannot treat all of your children the same. Why because they are individuals with different personalities, different temperaments, and different needs. Address each of them according to their individual abilities, and help them to understand their importance as an individual. Giving your children a sense of security and letting them know they are protected and a part of the family unit will keep them from seeking these assurances elsewhere. Don't ignore or try to explain away fears. Acknowledge them, admit them, and encourage them. Letting children know that you too are afraid, sometimes will allow them the freedom to meet their fears head on and be liberated in God rather than bound by the chains of men's expectations. Understanding the difference between discipline and punishment will allow you to more effectively develop responsible behavior in your child while communicating to them that you care.

Punishments are given as a penalty for an offense. It is usually handed out in hostility and frustration, and produces fear and guilt. Discipline, on the other hand, is used to train and to correct. Discipline must be fair. It needs to be explained to and understood by the child if it is to be effective. Discipline must also be prompt, and delivered as soon after the offense as possible. Finally, discipline must be terminal; no continued reminders, assured reacceptance. In an environment of discipline, the child will learn life's requirements in the context of love and concern. In an environment of true discipline, the child understands the importance of these requirements for their future, for God, and for society. Reminding ourselves frequently that our children are bound to make the same mistakes we did when we were young helps us to discard hypocritical ideas. Willingness to accept our children will fall short sometimes, and being tolerant of failure moves us toward acceptance which will keep us from giving up on them or tearing them down.

A soft word can turn away wrath, but a harsh word stirs up anger. (Proverbs 15:1)

Patience is a virtue. Reminding ourselves that our heavenly Father still loves us in spite of our failures will help us to think twice before shouting at our children so harshly for their mistakes. Reasonable, understandable discipline and parents, whose own behavior is consistent with the demands placed on the child, will lead to a parent child relationship of mutual love and respect. Last but definitely not least stay on your knees.

Don't just ask God to bless your children. Pray specific prayers on their behalf. Ask God to help them spiritually mature so they won't depart from His teachings. Pray that God will surround them with Godly friends and help them to make wise choices. Pray that their choices will encourage spiritual growth. Pray they will obey you and honor you because this is pleasing in the sight of the Lord.

Now, I know what you're thinking, we haven't seen any stories about Cheryl and Keith and how they raised their children. That's because many of these lessons have been learned by trial and error and even though our children are adults now, we are still parenting them as mentors. But there is one thing I know for sure marriage is the foundation of the family. If you strengthen your marriage you strengthen the family.

Don't allow your children to come between you and your spouse because children will grow up and leave and if you haven't nurtured and developed your marriage you will wake up one day and find you're lying next to a stranger. This isn't only the right thing for your relationship but it's the right thing for the children as well. Keith and I are each other's best friend. We are pals, buddies, road dawgs. Don't get to the point that the only time you and your spouse spend time together is with the children and then when you're alone you have nothing in common or all you can do is argue. Find ways to continue the romance in the quiet times. Relish the fact that you can find a babysitter on a Friday night and look for exciting new ways to romance one another.

Ladies don't let your husbands feel insignificant, disrespected, unloved, lonely, unappreciated, and resentful and angry because you show greater appreciation and attention for your children than you do them. Invest in your husband's stock by speaking about things you admire about him with the children and with others. Be spontaneous. Take a special trip or a special night out just for the two of you. Take a drive alone at the spur of the moment. I tell you these are some of the most special times Keith and I have. I often tell him it's just me and him against the world.

Keeping marriage and children in perspective will lift a huge burden off the relationship and lead to a healthier, happier, lifestyle.

Pray Without Ceasing

God why doesn't he understand? Make him understand? Make him do what he's supposed to do. Why is he so stubborn and bullheaded? Why doesn't he listen? God change his heart and mind. Make him that kind of man he should be.

I remember praying these kinds of prayers for Keith. I wanted God to change him into the kind of man I thought he should be. Problem is it wasn't my place to determine what that was. God had a plan for His life and only He had the right to determine the kind of man Keith should become. My prayers were full of meaningless words; words that had no significance with God. The Bible calls this vain repetition – babbling. Being specific rather than praying general, vague prayers presents specific requests to God. The more focused my prayers, the more direct my responses.

Through careful study and meditation on the Word of God rather than merely reading and quoting scriptures I felt suited my needs for the day, I have learned some valuable lessons about prayer including what it takes for them to become effectual and fervent.

Prayer is a gift of God through which needs might be met. It's a process of continually asking, seeking, and knocking. It's a time for making requests known to God while you wait for his answer to flow back to you in a revelatory word from the Lord. Receiving this revelatory word can only led you to the development of an attitude of having the mind of Christ, abiding in Him as He abides in us.

Earnest, intense, serious, prayer, the kind that presses on relentlessly is the kind of prayer that the Apostle Paul admonished us to pursue. But earnest prayer can only be entered into when the conscience is clear and the heart is forgiving. Jesus said our trespasses keep our prayers from being heard and answered. And if we don't forgive others we then cannot be forgive of God.

Un-forgiveness puts up a wall in our relationship with God. It gives the enemy the right to torment us. That torment can be manifested in many ways; financial problems, fear and anxiety, health problems. I had to learn how to forgive Keith, truly forgive him, for harsh words, acts of indifference, and anything else he may have done whether knowingly or unknowingly. He had to do the same because it was the only way we could develop an atmosphere conducive for God to answer our prayers. We had to release any bitterness, resentment, hostility, or un-forgiveness we may have been harboring in the deep places of our souls; the places that only God could reach. We had to learn how to apologize when we were wrong. Both of us had to be active in the forgiveness process because leaving the door open for the enemy to intervene in our marriage would bring in levels of spiritual strongholds and hindrances the magnitude of which we would not be strong enough to overcome.

Discipline in prayer is what separates the mature Christian from the immature babe in Christ. Praying out of discipline rather than out of feelings or emotions like I had done so many times before only equates to empty, meaningless prayers that have no hope of ever being answered because they are not in the will of God.

By studying and meditating on Scripture we have learned that the only way your prayers can be effective is if you pray His Word back to Him. You see, we each have angels assigned to us waiting to minister to us, waiting to work on our behalf. But the only way they'll shift into action is when they hear God's word. When these words are spoken, even commanded, God is obligated to answer and fulfill His promises. His Word cannot return to Him void. Remembering God wants to give us good gifts that are in line with His will we approached God with confidence, asking boldly for what we wanted according to His will. We had to stop being timid when we prayed for our marriage. We no longer prayed just to get by; We prayed to thrive in our marriage.

To truly experience a marriage of purpose, a marriage ordered by God, a marriage that was rewarding, we needed to seek God's face. We needed to listen for His divine revelation on the subject of marriage. His manual, the Bible, was the only course of action. It was our refuge. Everything God had to say about men and women, husbands and wives, and marriage relationships would be found here. And if we're obedient to the roadmap our final destination will be a marriage of lifelong contentment. Scouring scriptures and absorbing each word like a sponge we began to see ourselves and our marriage in a different light; our strengths and our weaknesses, our personal shortcomings and our personal virtues. Rather than praying for changes in each other we began praying for changes in ourselves decreeing and declaring the Words that God said about us and each other. We were fervently seeking God's face for divine wisdom on when to speak and when to be silent; His word of knowledge on the divine order of families and the actions and behaviors honoring to Him in our marriage.

First and foremost we loved God. Our marriage became less about pleasing ourselves and more about pleasing Him. We each made our relationship with Jesus our top priority -- over our marriage – and we encouraged each other to do the same. When we both had Jesus and His love in the forefront, His love filled our marriage and empowered us to love each other more. We looked to God for security and self-esteem – not one another. We prayed to have the wisdom and strength to rely on God every day rather than putting unnecessary pressure on each other. I prayed that Keith would love the Bible and read it regularly, hate sin, love to pray, welcome Christian community in his life, love to worship, understand the significance of fighting for his family spiritually, and be a mighty man of God. I asked God to fill him with the Holy Spirit each day and make him a great leader in our marriage. Lo and behold our pastor began an entire series entitled "Fight to Win" that taught men about fighting for their families. Look at God. Here was a man of God my husband truly respected and listened to teaching on the very things I was praying for! To God be the Glory!

The first time he came into the room and prayed for me before he went to work touched me so deeply there weren't words to say. Each morning when I awoke to find him asking for the grace to treat me as well as Jesus treated him I was obligated to pray for him in the same way. His prayers for the humility he needed to be a gentle leader in our marriage laid the foundation for me to make sure I was in proper alignment with the will of God. He prayed for peace in our home, and maturity for both of us as we deal with disagreements. He asked God to strengthen my faith; to help me love to pray, worship, and read the Bible, to convict me of sin and to make me quick to repent, and to help me follow where God was leading us both in our marriage. Keith wanted to see me as God sees me and to appreciate the gift I was to him. Most challenging was the ability to be obedient to the will of God for our marriage. Years of walking on a darkly lit path eventually gave way to a more enlightened road of mutual submission and respect.

As we continue our journey together in holy matrimony we now pray for our marriage's mission. Asking God for the ability to see beyond just the two of us but to see instead the greater world and how our marriage can be a blessing in it. We want God to use our marriage to touch other people's lives in positive ways, contributing to God's kingdom on earth. We pray for a vision of how God wants to use us to serve others. We have been petitioning God to show us an area of life we both are passionate about and could impact together leading us to ministry opportunities in that area. Our marriage is fully committed to God as we ask Him to constantly show us how we can best balance our time, resources, and skills for God's kingdom.

The prayers at the end of this book will help you develop a prayer life for your marriage that is honoring to God. It will cause you to understand what God values most in marriages. You'd be surprised it may not be what you think. God's ways are not our ways and His thoughts are not our thoughts.

As your prayer life matures you may also find it helpful if you and your spouse come to agreement on fasting for your marriage and family as well. You'll find during these times you are able to truly be ministered to by the Holy Spirit.

Remember the effectual fervent prayer of the righteous yields a lot.

Epilogue: Happily Ever After

God isn't finished with us yet. Sculpting us; painstakingly chipping away at us as a sculptor does his masterpiece so is God shaping and reshaping us ultimately to confirm us into the likeness of His son. We've accepted Jesus as the person in charge of our marriage so, if Jesus is willing to work with each of us and love us in spite of our shortcomings, then who are we not to follow His lead. Twenty-four-seven, seven-days-a-week that's the commitment we've made to God and each other for the transformation of our union. Consistently pushed to look at our selfishness as we are continually developing into the character of Jesus Christ makes us see one another as God does.

This seed of faith in His ability has been planted in our marriage. Like any seed it must be watered and cultivated in order to grow. Continuous study of the

Word of God is the soil in which the seed is planted and prayer waters it each day. Stirred to pray for one another because more than anything we each are concerned about the others walk with the Lord our prayers focus on the will of God for our spouses' life first and foremost..

Reading God's Word reminds me Keith is made in God's image and so am I. Each time I look at him watching TV, or stare at him across a dinner table I look into the eyes of a man made in the image of God. This divine image chips away at even the strongest of walls that may have been built between us and we are instantly realigned to God's order. You really can't argue with the image of God for too long. Released perverted standards of marriage from a fallen world allowed us to open up to a new set of standards – God's standards.

Realization that the primary purpose of our marriage is to model God's love to a world that now believes love is only for a moment has motivated us to live 2 Corinthians 5:9 daily. We make it our goal to please Him and over time God's grace has become visible in our marriage not only to us but to those touched by our relationship.

In the beginning it was rough, but I actively waited for my husband. I prepared, anticipated … and hoped. My life didn't begin when I met Keith. I already had a life, a life I was readying and expecting to share with another. I couldn't wait for a husband to complete me. He would be my complement, and I his. I knew God could fulfill me; it wasn't going to be my husband's job to meet my every need. Daily, I made choices to create a life that another would want to become a part of — and had the faith that one day, a husband would join that life. When you have longed and hoped for someone for such a long time and he's finally here and real, the joy in having your heart's desire doesn't soon diminish. Our lives are now intertwined. We read, play, laugh and discuss — together.

When we constantly invest in each other, our love is abundant. However, when love and attention are lopsided, we both suffer. If I'm sacrificing and Jeremy doesn't notice, I naturally feel entitled to point it out to him. This helps very little. I'm learning to use honest words to tell him how I feel and I'm learning not to expect him to read my mind. With that approach, he tends to respond to what I am saying. We both want our marriage to succeed, be filled with joy and grow. In this goal, we are intentional and dedicated. Our marriage was a decision of our wills, with the willingness to love in the ordinary occurences of life and not just the grand events.

We are both becoming more teachable. Humbling, yes, but if I want to learn to love my husband the way he needs and not the way I think he needs, I first have to listen. Listening requires me to hear his words and trust what he is saying. Believing we each want the best for each other is crucial.

Love is real to me. It is real when my tired husband returns from work with a desire to just lie down for a few minutes but instead he chooses to take me to our favorite restaurant when I'm completely content in knowing that I'm worth the effort. Love is real to me when he makes his way toward the pots on the stove where he finds his favorite meal cooking, the aroma permeating the air with a scent so tantalizing it makes his mouth water. Then he finds out I waited for him to come home so we could share a meal together. This is real love.

There is a delicate balance to the transitioning that takes place in a marriage. Hard work is part of the transition.

Happily-ever-after can only occur when God is the foundation of your union. The good news is if God has not truly been the foundation of your marriage it's not too late. Allow Him to pick up the broken pieces and mend them back together. Allow him to be God in your marriage.

And, together with God, Keith and Cheryl shall live a life happily ever after and you can too.

Prayers

PRAYERS FOR COMMUNICATION IN MARRIAGE

Heavenly Father we come to you in the name of Jesus•
We confess that our words will no longer be quick from
our mouth; we won't be hasty in our heart to utter
anything before God according to Ecclesiastes 5:2.We
will not consider ourselves religious and yet not keep a
tight rein on our tongue; we deceive ourselves making
our religion worthless according to James 1:26. We
decree and declare that according to Proverbs 15:2 our
tongues are wise commending knowledge, and not the
mouth of the fool that gushes folly. Our hearts will be
righteous and weigh its answers, not the mouth of the
wicked that gushes evil because we will have to give
account on the day of judgment for every careless word
have spoken. For by our words we will be acquitted,
and by our words we will be condemned. We will walk
in wisdom so that our hearts guide our mouth, and our
lips promote instruction according to Proverbs 16:23.
Being made righteous by the Son of God our lips will
know what is fitting, and our mouths will not be
wicked knowing only what is perverse according to
Proverbs 10:29. We confess that our answers will turn
away wrath, not harsh words stirring up anger knowing

reckless words pierce like a sword, but the tongue of the wise brings healing according to Proverbs 12:18. Because we seek after wisdom we fear the Lord and shun evil, we are not as a fool hotheaded and reckless because according to Proverbs 14:16-17 a quick-tempered man does foolish things, and a crafty man is hated. We will be patient having great understanding, not quick-tempered displaying folly. We confess that by the power of the Holy Ghost we will no longer be angry stirring up dissension or hot-tempered committing many sins. We will not associate with those given to anger; or go with those that are hot-tempered, lest we learn their ways, and find a snare for ourselves according to Proverbs 22:24-25. We will men and women of knowledge using words with restraint, and a men and women of understanding and even-tempered. We won't speak in haste for Your Word says a fool gives full vent to his anger, but a wise man keeps himself under control. A fool's mouth is his undoing, and his lips are a snare to his soul. A fool finds no pleasure in understanding but delights in airing his own opinions. There is more hope for a fool than for him that speaks in haste because even a fool is thought wise if he keeps silent, and discerning if he holds his tongue The quiet words of the wise are more to be heeded than the shouts of a ruler of fools Instead, we will speak the truth in love, we will in all things grow up into him who is that Head, that is, Christ according to Ephesians 4:15.

By the power of the Holy Spirit we shall be wise in heart accepting commands, not chattering fool coming to ruin. God help us to avoid godless chatter, because those who indulge in it will become more and more ungodly according to 2 Timothy 2:16. Father God fix our tongues so that we will not have many words for in them sin is present, but cause us to hold our tongues in wisdom. In all prudence we will keep our knowledge to ourselves, not having the heart of fools blurting out folly. We decree and declare no unwholesome talk will come out of our mouths, but only what is helpful for building others up according to their needs, that it may benefit those who listen according to Ephesians 4:29. Our tongues shall be righteous as choice silver, nourishing many, bringing healing as a tree of life not deceitful crushing the spirit Because we have been made righteous in Jesus the Christ our mouths shall be a fountain of life, and not like that of the wicked which violence overwhelms. Because the words of the wicked lie in wait for blood, but the speech of the upright rescues them Our lips shall be wise spreading knowledge, knowing what is fitting, and not what is perverse. We confess we would rather be poor walking blameless than a fool whose lips are perverse Holy Spirit help us to put away perversity from our mouth keeping corrupt talk far from our lips. Give us the wisdom to guard our lips for he who guards his lips guards his life, but he who speaks rashly will come to and he who guards his mouth and his tongue keeps himself from calamity. Father God search our hearts and help us to rid ourselves of all malice and deceit, hypocrisy, envy, and slander of every kind because a man of perverse heart does not prosper; and he whose tongue is deceitful falls into trouble. Cause our lips to be truthful and endure forever, for your Word says in Proverbs 12:19 a lying tongue lasts only a moment. Lord we acknowledge that you detest lying lips, but delight in men who are truthful so by the power of the Holy Ghost we command our mouths to speak what is true, for our lips detest wickedness. All of the words of our mouths are just; none of them is crooked or perverse because an honest answer is like a kiss on the lips. We will hate what is false, not being wicked bringing shame and disgrace. Above all, we will not swear—not by heaven or by earth or by anything else. Our "Yes" will be yes, and our "No," no, or we will be condemned according to James 5:12. Heavenly Father help us to be transparent before You and before our Spouse for according to Proverbs 28:13 he who conceals his sins does not prosper, but whoever confesses and renounces them finds mercy. Father remind us that the tongue has the power of life and death, and those who love it will eat its fruit. Keep us aware that words from a wise man's mouth are gracious, but a fool is consumed by his own lips. At the beginning his words are folly; at the end they are wicked madness—and the fool multiplies words according to Ecclesiastes 10:12-13. We confess we will be patient not a warrior. We will control our temper as the Spirit moves in our hearts.

We lay the sword of the Holy Spirit to the root of lying and we pull it up out of us and our marriage now and we render it powerless in our lives. In the name of Jesus we command miscommunication, false accusations, gossip, condemnation, exaggeration, excessive talking, profanity, slander, deception to leave us and our atmosphere. Go to Jesus now for disposal. We loose upon us and our marriage the Spirit of Truth which is Jesus and the Word of God. Come into us now in Jesus' name.

Father God we ask you to execute judgment on every evil spirit in our lives and atmosphere that will not give You glory. Execute judgment on every evil spirit that is disobedient to our command in the name of Jesus; According to John 14:14 we ask you to dispose of them as you will.

For thine is the Kingdom, and the Power, and the Glory. Amen.

PRAYERS FOR WISDOM IN MARRIAGE 1

Father God Your Word says a man's wisdom gives him patience and it is to his glory to overlook an offense. Lord we thank you love is not rude, self-seeking; easily angered, and keeps no record of wrongs and we decree and declare by the power of the Holy Ghost we will not see ourselves wise in our own eyes because there is more hope for a fool than for him. We confess that according to Your Word when pride comes, then comes disgrace, before his downfall a man's heart is proud, pride goes before destruction, and a haughty spirit before a fall. Pride only breeds quarrels, so we will be humble and maintain wisdom because humility comes before honor and wisdom is found in those who take advice. By the power of the Lamb that was slain, we will not play the fool and exalt ourselves, or plan evil. We will clap our hands over our mouth! For as churning the milk produces butter, and as twisting the nose produces blood, so stirring up anger produces strife according to Proverbs 30:32-33. Holy Spirit help us to discern what causes fights and quarrels among us. Your Word says they come from our desires that battle within us. We want something but don't get it. We kill and covet, but we cannot have what we want. We quarrel and fight according to James 4:1-2a. We confess that by the power of the Holy Spirit we will drop a matter before a dispute breaks out because starting a quarrel is like breaching a dam. We confess by the power of the Holy Ghost we will drop the matter before a dispute breaks out because your Word says it is to a man's honor to avoid strife, forgive us for being foolish and quick to quarrel because he who loves to quarrel loves sin. Heavenly father we come against the spirit that would have us biting and devouring each other for your Word says if we are not watchful we will be destroyed by each other. Guard our minds so we are not like the evil man trapped by his sinful talk for from the fruit of his lips a man is filled with good things as surely as the work of his hands rewards him. Forgive us for paying back evil for good because your word says evil will never leave our house. Finally, God help us to live in harmony with one another; be sympathetic, love as brothers, be compassionate and humble not repaying evil with evil or insult with insult, but with blessing, because to this we were called so that we may inherit a blessing. Help each of us put off falsehood and speak truthfully to our spouse, for we are all members of one body. Father God, in our anger we will not sin: We decree and declare we will not let the sun go down while we are still angry, and we will not give the devil a foothold sin. Holy Spirit act upon our hearts to get rid of all bitterness, rage and anger, brawling and slander, along with every form of malice... Therefore, ridding ourselves of all malice and all deceit, hypocrisy, envy, and slander of every kind according to 1 Peter 2:11. Lord, when we have been trapped by what we've said, ensnared by the words of our mouth, help us to free ourselves, since we have fallen into our spouse's hands: Help us to humble ourselves; press our plea with our neighbor spouse! Allow no sleep to our eyes, no slumber to our eyelids until we have been forgiven.

Right now God I lay the axe of the Holy Spirit to the root of the haughty spirit and I pull it up out of my spouse and our marriage and I render it powerless in our lives by the blood of Jesus Christ. I command that you leave us and our atmosphere now. Go to Jesus for disposal. I command all fruits of spirit of haughtiness pride, arrogance, contentiousness, control, critical thinking, dictatorialness, domination, egotism, judgmental attitudes, self righteousness, superiority, and rudeness to go from us now in the name of Jesus. I loose to come into us and our marriage the compassion of Christ, humbleness, modesty, humility, charity, love, submission, the righteousness of God, and gentleness.

Father God I ask according to John 14:14 that you execute judgment on every evil spirit in our lives and atmosphere that will not give you glory.

God continue to lead us not into temptation but deliver us from the evil on.

For Thine is the Kingdom and the Power and the Glory forever, Amen.

PRAYER FOR WISDOM IN MARRIAGE 2

Heavenly Father it's in the name of Jesus that we come to you now praying for new beginnings and new mercies in our marriage. Holy Spirit remind us to slander no one, to be peaceable and considerate, and to show true humility toward our spouse. Give us the grace to do everything without complaining or arguing, so that we may become blameless and pure, children of God without fault in a crooked and depraved generation shining like stars in the universe according to Philippians 2:14-15. Help us to make every effort to live in peace with our spouse and to be holy; for Your word says without holiness no one will see the Lord. Holy Spirit cover our hearts and our spirits so that no one misses the grace of God and that no bitter root grows up to cause trouble and defile our defile our marriage. According to your Word Lord God let us make every effort to do what leads to peace and to mutual edification in our relationship with one another. When our spouse curses us, we bless; when they persecute us, we endure it; when they slander us, we answer kindly according to 1 Corinthians 4:12-13a. Forgive us for having anything to do with foolish and stupid arguments, because according to Your word we know they produce quarrels. And the Lord's servant must not quarrel; instead, he must be kind to everyone, able to teach, not resentful. Give us the wisdom to gently instruct our spouses when they oppose us according to 2 Timothy 2:24 in the hope that God will grant them repentance leading them to a knowledge of the truth, and that they will come to their senses and escape from the trap of the devil, who has taken them captive to do his will. Father God, help us not to grieve the Holy Spirit of God, with whom you were sealed for the day of redemption. Increase our desire to get rid of all bitterness, rage and anger, brawling and slander, along with every form of malice. Give us the grace to be kind and compassionate to one another, forgiving each other, just as in Christ God forgave us. Help us to encourage one another and build each other up, just as in fact you are doing. Turn our hearts and minds to consider how we may spur our spouses on toward love and good deeds. Let us not give up on meeting together, as some are in the habit of doing, but let us encourage our spouse. We confess our love will be sincere hating what is evil; clinging to what is good. We will be devoted to one another and honor one another above ourselves. We decree and declare we will be imitators of God and live a life of love, just as Christ loved us and gave himself up for us as a fragrant offering and sacrifice to God. We will live a life worthy of the calling we have received as a married couple. We will be completely humble and gentle; patient, bearing with one another in love making every effort to keep the unity of the Spirit through the bond of peace according to Ephesians 4:1-3. Give us the pure wisdom that comes from heaven to be peace-loving, considerate, submissive, full of mercy and good fruit, impartial and sincere: peacemakers who sow in peace and raise a harvest of righteousness conducting ourselves in a manner worthy of the gospel of Christ whatever happens. By the might of the Ancient of Days we will aim for perfection, listen to our spouses appeal, be of one mind, and live in peace expecting the God of love and peace to be with us. As your Word instructs us in 2 Corinthians 13:11-12 we will greet one another with a holy kiss. Our gentleness will be evident to all. The Lord is near. Whatever you do, whether in word or deed, we will do it all in the name of the Lord Jesus, giving thanks to God the Father through Him. We plead the blood of Jesus as we demolish arguments and every pretension that sets itself up against the knowledge of God, and we take captive every thought to make it obedient to Christ according to 2 Corinthians 10:5.

I lay the axe of the Holy Spirit to the root of error and jealousy and I pull them up out of us and our marriage now and I render them powerless in our lives. In the name of Jesus, I command the spirits of contention, defensiveness, argumentativeness, error, non-submission, a non teachable spirit, confusion, indecision, double mindedness, anger, rage, cruelty, envy, extreme competitiveness, jealousy, hatred, spitefulness, and strife to leave me, my spouse, and our marriage. Go to Jesus now for disposal.

I loose upon our marriage the Spirit of truth, the Spirit of wise counsel, the Spirit of Wisdom, The Spirit of the fear of the Lord, singleness of mind, decisiveness, charity, the Love of God, mercy, kindness, and the compassion of Christ. I invite you to come into us and our marriage now in the name of Jesus.

Father God I ask you to execute judgment upon every evil spirit in our lives and atmosphere that won't give you glory.

Thank you Father for supplying all our needs according to Your riches in glory. Thank you for supplying all the needs for our marriage. Forgive us for transgressions of omission and commission and help us to forgive our spouse.

Lead us not into temptation and we thank you for delivering us from the evils that proceed out of the hearts of men.

You are great and greatly to be praised. Amen.

PRAYER FOR WISDOM IN MARRIAGE 3

Heavenly Father, we thank you that Your Word gives knowledge, instruction, wisdom, and understanding to all who pays attention to its truths. You promised to impart wisdom to us if we will listen to Your Words and attain unto Your wise counsels. We, therefore, enter Your presence with trust, knowing that You will give us wisdom according to II Chronicles 1:10. Heavenly Father, fill us with the spirit of wisdom so that we will be able to discern Your will. With You, Lord, there is both strength and wisdom according to Job 12:13. Father God give us the wisdom to encourage one another in our marriage and build each other up. Give us the conviction to pray continually; giving thanks in all circumstances, for this is Your will for us in Christ Jesus. Give us the grace to live in harmony with one another; to be sympathetic, to love as brothers, to be compassionate and humble. Holy Sprit lead us to not repay evil with evil or insult with insult, but with blessing, because to this we were called so that we may inherit a blessing.

Heavenly Father, thank You for sending Jesus who represents Your power and wisdom to us. Because we are in Him – and desire to always abide in Him. He has been made unto us wisdom, and righteousness, sanctification, and redemption. In His name we pray. Amen.

PRAYER FOR RESOLVING CONFLICT

Heavenly father I pray that my spouse and I have tender hearts and wisdom that we commit ourselves to come together in a spirit of humility and reconciliation thinking only of the health of our marriage and not our individual interests. Search us God and know our hearts; test us and know our anxious thoughts. See if there is any offensive way in us and lead us in the way everlasting. Give us the wisdom to accept Your words and store up your commands within us, turning our ears to wisdom and applying our hearts to understanding. According to Proverbs 2:1-5 we call out for insight and cry aloud for understanding, we look for it as for silver and search for it as for hidden treasure expecting that we will understand the fear of the Lord and find the knowledge of God. We will not be wise in our own eyes; we fear the Lord and shun evil. Forgive us God for doing things out of selfish ambition or vain conceit, we make ourselves humble before you and ask for the grace to consider others better than ourselves. We decree and declare we will not look only to our own interests, but also to the interests of spouse. We confess our minds have not always been prepared for action; we are not always self-controlled; but we pray for the power of the Holy Spirit and set our hope fully on the grace to be given us when Jesus Christ is revealed. By the grace of God we commit to handle ourselves with maturity —being quick to listen and slow to speak according to James 1:19—reaching for the goal of continually trying to better understand each other. According to 1 Corinthians 13:11 when I was a child, I talked like a child, I thought like a child. When I became a man, I put childish ways behind me. We will stop thinking like children and in regard to evil we will be infants, but in our thinking will be adults. Father, forgive us for speaking the truth in love respectfully honoring each other's feelings. God no unwholesome talk will come out of our mouths, but only what is helpful for building our spouse up according to their needs, that it may benefit them. Father, forgive us for allowing our discussions to escalate into yelling or name-calling; provoking each other with sarcasm, innuendos, and rudeness. According to Proverbs 4:24 we will put away perversity from our mouth keeping corrupt talk far from our lips because he who guards his lips guards his life, but he who speaks rashly will come to ruin. God we decree according to Proverbs 8:7-8 our mouth speaks what is true all of the words of our mouth are just; none of them is crooked or perverse for it is written the tongue has the power of life and death, and those who love it will eat its fruit. Holy Spirit engulf us and incline us to love, truly love according to 1

Corinthians 13:5 which says love is not rude, it is not self-seeking; it is not easily angered; it keeps no record of wrongs. Holy Spirit impress upon our hearts to mean what we say. Let our integrity guide us. May any false witness against us perish, and whoever listens to him be destroyed forever according to Proverbs 21:28. Our "Yes" will be "Yes", and our "No," "No"; for anything beyond this comes from the evil one. Father God let everything even our discussions be done in a fitting and orderly way; according to Proverbs 4:25-26 our eyes look straight ahead, our gaze is fixed directly before us. We will not swerve to the right or the left. According to 1 Peter 4:7 the end of all things is near. Therefore we will be clear minded and self-controlled so that you can pray. Holy Spirit help us to be accurate, truthful, and realistic in what we say help us to express our own feelings over matters and not be judgmental. Because according to Matthew 7:1-2 we should not judge, or we too will be judged. For in the same way we judge others, we will be judged, and with the measure we use, it will be measured to us. We will not accuse our spouse of feelings they may or may not have because the heart of the righteous weighs its answers, but the mouth of the wicked gushes evil. We will each look for the plank in our own eye rather than the speck in our spouse's for all a man's ways seem innocent to him, but motives are weighed by the Lord. Heavenly Father forgive us for not readily apologizing and sincerely asking for forgiveness for whatever way that we have hurt our spouse and for whatever tension we've caused in our marital relationship by our behavior for Your Word says in Matthew 6:14 if we forgive our spouse when they sin against you, our heavenly Father will also forgive us. But if you do not forgive their sins, our Father will not forgive your sins. Help us to forgive. Holy Spirit, incline our hearts to forgive each other as Christ has forgiven us. Keep us mindful not to remind our spouse of the pain for which we've said we've forgiven them. And we'll make daily choices not to dwell on those painful thoughts in the future. We confess to be peacemakers, so we will be called sons of God. We will make every effort to do what leads to peace and mutual edification. According to 2 Corinthians 10:5 We will demolish arguments and every pretension that sets itself up against the knowledge of God, and we take captive every thought to make it obedient to Christ. We will be kind and compassionate to one another, forgiving each other, just as in Christ God forgave us. We decree and declare that we will bear with each other and forgive whatever grievances we have against one another forgiving as the Lord has forgiven us. In the name of Jesus we will confess our sins to each other and pray for each other so that we may be healed because the prayers of the righteous availeth much. We will give thanks for what we've learned about our relationship with each other.

We will each ask God to bless our spouse and help us to be a blessing to them knowing that is our mission. We commit our marriage to the Lord so our plans will succeed. According to <u>Philippians 1:9-10</u> we pray that our love may abound more and more in knowledge and depth of insight, so that we may be able to discern what is best and may be pure and blameless until the day of Christ. The peace of Christ will rule in our hearts, since as members of one body we are called to peace. May the God of peace, who through the blood of the eternal covenant brought back from the dead our Lord Jesus, that great Shepherd of the sheep, equip us with everything good for doing his will, and may he work in us what is pleasing to him, through Jesus Christ. Amen

PRAYERS FOR MARRIAGE

Father God in the name of Jesus we come to you now decreeing and declaring that our children will listen to what we say and treasure our commands. We confess that we will tune our ears to wisdom, and concentrate on understanding crying out for insight, and asking for understanding. We will search for them as we would for silver; we will seek them like hidden treasures that by the power of the Holy Spirit we will then understand what it means to fear the Lord, and we will gain knowledge of God. Father God we bless you name. We praise you. We lift you up. We magnify you. God we confess that we will trust in you with all our hearts; we won't depend on our own understanding. We will seek your will in all we do so that you can show us which path to take. By the power of the Holy Spirit we decree and declare that wise choices will watch over us and understanding will keep us safe. Wisdom will save us from evil people, from those whose words are twisted. God we will never let loyalty and kindness leave us! They will be tied around our necks as a reminder. They will be written deep within our hearts and we will guard our heart above all else, for it determines the course of our life. Amen.

FORGIVENESS PRAYER

Heavenly Father, we come to You now in the Name of our Lord and Savior Christ Jesus. Father God we confess we will speak the truth in love, growing in every way more and more like Christ, who is the head of his body, the church. We decree and declare we won't use foul or abusive language and that everything we say will be good and helpful, so that your words will be an encouragement to our spouse who hears them. We will not speak without thinking but rather our words will be godly and encourage our spouse. We will not be fools destroyed by their lack of common sense. Our lips will be godly and speak helpful words, not wicked speaking perverse words. Father, help me us to let go of all bitterness and resentment. You are the One Who binds up and heals the broken-hearted. We receive Your anointing that breaks and destroys every yoke of bondage. we receive healing by faith according to Your Word, Isaiah 53:5, "and with His stripes we are healed". Thank You for sending us Your Holy Spirit, we acknowledge the Holy Spirit as our wonderful Counselor Thank You for helping us work out our salvation with fear and trembling, for it is You, Father, Who works in us to will and to act according to Your good purpose.

In the Name of Jesus, we choose to forgive our spouse. We choose to live a life of forgiveness because You have forgiven us. We repent of all resentments, bitterness, rage, anger, brawling, and slander, along with every form of malice. We desire to be kind and compassionate to others, forgiving them, just as in Christ You forgave us. With the help of the Holy Spirit, we make every effort to live in peace with all men and to be holy, for we know that without holiness no one will see You. We will watch and pray that we will not enter into temptation or cause others to stumble. Thank You, Heavenly Father, that You watch over Your Word to perform it and that whom the Son has set free is free indeed. we declare that we have overcome resentment and bitterness by the Blood of the Lord Jesus Christ and by the Word of our testimony. Amen!

PRAYER FOR FINANCES

Heavenly Father, in the Name of Jesus Christ, We praise Your Holy Name. Thank You Lord, You are our God; we will exalt You. we will give thanks to Your Name; for You have worked wonders, plans formed long ago, with perfect faithfulness according to Isaiah 25:1.God we decree and declare that we will love people and use money rather that loving money and using people for the love of money is the root of all kinds of evil. And some people, craving money, have wandered from the true faith and pierced themselves with many sorrows. Heavenly Father, in Your son Jesus' name, we pray Your Word over our finances and we thank You for manifesting Your Word in our life according to 3 John 1:2; "Beloved, I wish above all things that thou mayest prosper and be in health, even as thy soul prospereth; "But thou shall remember the Lord thy God: for it is He that giveth thee power to get wealth, that He may establish His covenant which He swore unto thy fathers, as it is this day." According to Deut. 8:1; "...but shall believe that those things which he saith shall come to pass; he shall have whatsoever he saith." According to Mark 11:23; "And these are they which sown on good ground; such as hear the Word and receive it, and bring forth fruit, some thirty fold, some sixty, and some a hundred." According to Mark 4:20; "He that keepeth his mouth keepeth his life: but he that openeth wide his lips shall have destruction." According to Proverbs 13:3; "I can do all things through Christ which strengthen me." "But my God shall supply all your needs according to His riches in glory by Christ Jesus." according to Philippians 4:13, 19; "But this I say, he which soweth sparingly shall reap also sparingly; and he which soweth bountifully shall reap also bountifully." "Every man according as he purposeth in his heart, so let him give; not grudgingly, or of necessity: for God loveth a cheerful giver." "And God is able to make all grace abound toward you; that ye, always having all sufficiency in all things, may abound to every good work.", according to 2 Corinthians 9:6-8.

We decree and declare that You, who takes care of us will supply all our needs from your glorious riches, which have been given to us in Christ Jesus. We will not worry about everyday life—whether we have enough food and drink, or enough clothes to wear. because life is more than food, and our body more than clothing We will be content with whatever we have knowing how to live on almost nothing or with everything learning the secrets of living in every situation, whether it is with a full stomach or empty, with plenty or little for we can do everything through

Christ, who gives us strength. Father God we give thanks to You, for you are good! And your faithful love endures forever. For everyone has sinned; we all fall short of God's glorious standard. But God showed his great love for us by sending Christ to die for us while we were still sinners. Now God we confess that we have not worked at living in peace with everyone, but with the grace of God we will work at living a holy life, for those who are not holy will not see the Lord. We will look after each other so that neither of us fails to receive the grace of God. We will watch out that no poisonous root of bitterness grows up to trouble us, and corrupt us. We will forgive our spouse when they sin against us, you heavenly Father will forgive us. We will not refuse to forgive others, for you will not forgive our sins. Amen.

PRAYER FOR HUSBANDS AND WIVES

Heavenly Father, I (we) come to You now in the Name of my (our) Lord and Savior Christ Jesus declaring that wives will be wise women building their houses, not foolish tearing them down with their own hands. We confess that husbands and wives will submit themselves one to the other out of reverence to Christ according to Ephesians 5:21 will not be quarrelsome like a constant dripping or ill-tempered wife for Your word says it is• better to live in a desert or on a corner of the roof than share a house with her. Your Word says restraining her is like restraining the wind or grasping oil with the hand according to Proverbs 27:15-16 God we decree and declare Wives, be submissive to their husbands so that, if any of them do not believe the word, they may be won over without words by the behavior of their wives, when they see the purity and reverence of their lives. We confess their beauty will not come from outward adornment, such as braided hair and wearing of gold jewelry and fine clothes. Instead, it will be that of their inner self, the unfading beauty of a gentle and quiet spirit, which is of great worth in God's sight

By the power of the Holy Spirit we decree and declare Husbands, in the same way will be considerate as they live with their wives, helping with the children, helping with household duties, and seeking to assist their wives. They will treat their wives with respect as the weaker partner and as heirs with them of the gracious gift of life, understanding that not to do so will hinder their prayers according to 1 Peter 3:7. Husbands will love their wives as Christ loves the church and died for it according to Ephesians 5:25.

Heavenly Father, we ask You to rebuke any plans of the enemy to keep this family from being together. We know Lord that satan comes to steal, kill and destroy but we stand firm and confident knowing that he has no power over You, Lord Jesus.

Thank You, Father, for hearing our prayer on behalf of husbands and wives as we strive for the love of God to reign supreme in their homes, and for the peace of God to act as umpire in all situations.

As for me and my house, we will serve the Lord. May our family know that You are Lord, spirit, soul and body and that you watch over Your Word to perform it, in Jesus Name we pray. Amen.